Roots of Freedom

ROOTS OF FREEDOM
A Primer on Modern Liberty

By John W. Danford

ISI Books
Wilmington, Delaware

Cataloging-in-Publication Data

Danford, John W.
Roots of freedom : a primer on modern liberty / by John W.
Danford. — 2nd ed. —Wilmington, Del. : ISI Books, 2000

p.   cm.
Includes index.

ISBN   1-882926-90-0 (pbk.)
1. Liberty—History. 2. Political science—Philosophy. I. Title

JC585 .D36 2000   2002103505
323/ .09—dc21   CIP

INTERIOR BOOK DESIGN BY MARJA WALKER
COVER DESIGN BY JOHN M. VELLA

Published in the United States by:
        ISI Books
        Intercollegiate Studies Institute
        P.O. Box 4431
        Wilmington, DE 19807-0431
        www.isibooks.org

To Will, David, and Nadia

ROOTS OF FREEDOM

PREFACE

So short a book should not have so long a list of people the author is obliged to thank. But this primer was begun a very long time ago, during the Cold War, and over the years of its development I have benefited from discussions and direct suggestions from many friends and colleagues whose help I would like to acknowledge. My first debt is to Radio Liberty and its director (in 1988), S. Enders Wimbush, whose idea it was that I compose and broadcast short, clear introductions to the great thinkers of the Western political tradition of liberty, so that listeners behind the iron curtain could have a taste of the ideas which undergird free societies.

Friends from my Houston days (only one of whom remains in Houston) gave generously of their time: John Ettling, David Brady, Tony Sirignano, and Laura Scalia. I used part of a year away from teaching to work on *Roots of Freedom,* and that time was made possible by a generous grant from the Lynde and Harry Bradley Foundation. My colleagues at Liberty Fund, Inc., where I spent 1996-97 as a Visiting Scholar, were kind enough to give of their time and expertise, in some cases reading the entire manuscript: Bill Dennis, Emilio Pacheco, Todd Breyfogle, David Bovenizer, George Martin, Steve Ealy, Hans Eicholz, John Alvis, and my fellow Senior Research Fellow, Nick Capaldi. I would also like to thank the members of Liberty Fund's Board of Directors. I owe a special debt to Professor Robert Eden of Hillsdale College, who was outside reader for the manuscript and at whose suggestion I added an entire chapter (chapter 7).

The staff at ISI Books—Jeff Nelson, Chris Briggs, Claudia Pasquantonio, and Brooke Haas—was efficient, courteous, and professional in ever respect, and it was a pleasure to work with them. I am indebted to Kim Dennis for putting me in touch with ISI Books in the first place. Finally, I owe a debt that can never be repaid to my wife, Karen Pawluk Danford, who reads and improves everything I write. I dedicate this little book to our three wonderful children, Will, David, and Nadia, in the hope that they and their chldren will live with the precious blessings of freedom.

INTRODUCTION

On June 6, 1995, *The Wall Street Journal* published an editorial entitled "RFE/RL R. I. P." to mark the downsizing of Radio Free Europe and Radio Liberty. These twin broadcasting services, launched by the United States early in the Cold War and headquartered in Munich, had for decades beamed radio transmissions into the communist East Bloc nations and the former Soviet Union, in an attempt to provide independent Western-style news and analysis to the peoples locked behind the Iron Curtain.

Terms like "East Bloc" and "Iron Curtain" already have a quaint ring to them, and will soon require special explanation. Yet only a little more than a decade ago, next door to the advanced industrial nations that make up what was then called the Free World, scores of millions of people lived under communist tyrannies that denied them free speech, the freedom to own property, and even the freedom to emigrate. How quickly we forget.

In addition to acting as an objective news service for subjects of communist regimes, the two radio services

tried to give these people access to the ideas that formed
the roots of free societies. Communist rulers knew how
corrosive free thought would be to the Iron Curtain—
they imposed stiff penalties for listening to the broadcasts,
and lavished megawatts to jam them.

In 1988 the director of Radio Liberty, S. Enders
Wimbush, asked me to write a series of articles for the
broadcasts. He requested brief and clear accounts of the
thought of philosophers such as John Locke and Adam
Smith for broadcast on Radio Free Europe and Radio
Liberty.

As I began writing, I realized that my listeners needed
more than an overview of the great individual philosophers; they also needed a description of the historical
periods and movements, such as the Protestant
Reformation or the American founding, which influenced the growth of free societies. Locke and Adam
Smith—along with less-known philosophers such as
Machiavelli, Hobbes, Hume, and Montesquieu—had
indeed planted and watered the roots of our modern free
societies, but those roots thrived or withered depending
on the historical climate.

Broadcasts of the series began in September of 1989.
Time passed; the Berlin Wall fell; and the East Bloc was no
more.

I took considerable pride in the series of articles, but,
thinking they had served their purpose, thought little

more about them. Some individuals, however, who had heard or knew about the series, pointed out that it would be of value to people outside the former communist world. They suggested that I should adapt the series to the citizens of free societies who wanted to know more about the philosophical and historical foundations of political freedom. The articles that were once broadcast beyond the Iron Curtain became the chapters of this book.

Many years ago I had the privilege of teaching in "the core," as it was called, in the undergraduate college at the University of Chicago. I have never forgotten the opening lines of one of the collections of readings we used, a book called *The People Shall Judge*:

> This book expresses the faith of one American college in the usefulness of liberal education to American democracy. If the United States is to be a democracy, its citizens must be free. If citizens are to be free, they must be their own judges. If they are to judge well, they must be wise. Citizens may be born free; they are not born wise. Therefore, the business of liberal education in a democracy is to make free men wise.[1]

It seems to me that those words are, if anything, more important at the end of the twentieth century than when they were written decades ago. For despite the end of the Cold War and the apparent triumph of the principles of

---

[1] *The People Shall Judge* (Chicago: University of Chicago Press, 1949), p. v.

liberal democracy, societies such as the United States are vulnerable to a danger that was scarcely foreseen in 1949, when *The People Shall Judge* first appeared: the collapse of the belief in human nature. Free societies such as ours were once thought to be best precisely because they were in accord with human nature. Thus free societies are especially vulnerable to developments that undermine the notion of human nature itself. That collapse, which I will describe fully later, has become increasingly apparent in the twentieth century—a century that has not been favorable for free societies.

What is a free society? People would surely differ, but what is meant here is a society in which human beings are not "born into" a place—a caste or an occupation, for example—but are free to own property, to raise children, to earn a living, to think, to worship, to express political views, and even to emigrate if desired, and to do so without seeking permission from a master. Obviously no human being lives without constraints of many sorts, including physical constraints (gravity, or the need to eat). The moral obligation to care for offspring or for aged parents, for example, has always limited human freedom. But for much of human history, including recent history, most human beings have lived in circumstances more constraining than those that would be acceptable to, say, someone who lives in the United States—a free society—today.

Free societies have been rare in human history. They

also seem to be fragile—more fragile than were the dynasties or empires of the ancient world, or even the great republics of antiquity, Sparta and Rome. Why they are rare and fragile is worth serious reflection. As the twenty-first century dawns, there are still relatively few free societies. Why are they so rare in human history? This question can be approached indirectly, by thinking about the topic of liberal education.

Three Obstacles

Liberal education, to the ancients who first conceived it, was the education appropriate for a *free man*, that is, for a human being who was not enslaved. But of course there is more than one kind of slavery: one can be enslaved to a master, but one can also be enslaved by necessity—there is no freedom for a person who has to work every waking minute just to survive. In the ancient world the free man or gentleman was free precisely because someone else was enslaved: the free man was free because he did not need to work for a living. This helps to explain why free societies have been so rare in history. For many centuries only a few could be free because their freedom depended on the enslavement of others. Genuine freedom requires some escape from economic necessity.

By about the end of the eighteenth century, economic necessity had ceased to be the main obstacle to freedom in many places. The productive powers of emerging com-

mercial societies allowed a substantial part of the population to enjoy some leisure. In 1776 Adam Smith, the
Scottish moral philosopher, published *An Inquiry into the
Nature and Causes of the Wealth of Nations*. The introduction
and plan of the work contains this observation:

> Among the savage nations of hunters and fishers, every
> individual who is able to work, is more or less employed
> in useful labour, and endeavors to provide…for himself,
> or such of his family or tribe as are either too old, or too
> young, or too infirm to go a hunting and fishing. Such
> nations, however, are so miserably poor, that…they are
> frequently reduced…to the necessity sometimes of
> directly destroying, and sometimes of abandoning their
> infants, their old people, and those afflicted with lingering
> diseases, to perish with hunger, or to be devoured by wild
> beasts.[2]

Smith went on to contrast this state of affairs with the
condition of emerging commercial societies such as
Britain:

> Among civilized and thriving nations, on the contrary,
> though a great number of people do not labour at
> all…yet the produce of the whole labour of the society is
> so great, that all are often abundantly supplied, and a
> workman, even of the lowest and poorest order, if he is

[2]Adam Smith, *An Inquiry into the Nature and Causes of the Wealth of Nations*
(Indianapolis: Liberty Classics, 1976), p. lviii.

frugal and industrious, may enjoy a greater share of the necessaries and conveniencies of life than it is possible for any savage to acquire.[3]

Certainly by the twentieth century, if not by 1776, economic advances in commercial societies had overcome one of the great obstacles to liberty.

Economic progress, however, though necessary, is not sufficient to achieve a free society. Certain political arrangements are equally indispensable. A tyrannical regime may oppress individuals even when they live in relatively prosperous circumstances. Thus we must add some notion of individual rights to our definition of a free society: the individual must be *prior* to the state or community. It follows that government powers must be *limited*. Of course, the most despotic of modern states have paid lip service to the notion of individual rights and limited government, but free societies have established institutional checks and balances to make the notion a reality. One such check is the separation of governmental powers. As James Madison said in *The Federalist Papers*, "the accumulation of all powers, legislative, executive, and judiciary, in the same hands, whether of one, a few, or many, and whether hereditary, self-appointed, or elective, may justly be pronounced the very definition of tyranny."[4]

[3] *Ibid.*

[4] James Madison, *The Federalist Papers*, (New York: The New American Library, 1961) No. 47, p. 301.

To the separation of powers (which implies rule of law and independent judiciary) one might add the rights of revolution and emigration as good indicators of the political arrangements of a free society. Students of political science would point to the British and American constitutional orders as the clearest examples of the political arrangements consistent with a free society.

But while economic sufficiency and freedom from oppression are necessary for a free society, they are not enough. They form, so to speak, the physical requirements of a free society, but there is still need of a spirit. And so we return to the dilemma mentioned above as particularly troubling in recent decades: our belief in human nature.

A free society requires order, and order depends on restraint: yet it seems that the only kind of restraint compatible with genuine freedom is self-restraint. Thus a free society cannot long exist if its citizens do not consider self-restraint a virtue. And the twentieth century has given us ample reason for concern about this most difficult requirement.

It is in some of the most "advanced" of the industrial countries, with liberal constitutions and economic prosperity, that we most easily see the lack of self-restraint. The hedonism of individual pleasure-seeking, the sense that there is no limit to what is permitted in the name of individual fulfillment or "actualization," the disappearance of any sense of obligations—these are early warnings of a free society's decay.

The sexual revolution, which began in the 1960s, has highlighted this rather starkly in the United States and Western Europe. The rate of illegitimacy has soared over the past three decades, leading to all the turmoil that appears when the civilizing force of the family disappears. Teenage boys who have never had a father to teach them civilized behavior—which requires, at a minimum, learning how to control anger—torment inner city neighborhoods in gangs. Not surprisingly, this has turned cities or parts of cities into savage and fearsome places, where the idea of a free society is foreign.

Although most suburbs have not experienced the torrent of lawlessness common in inner cities, there is no question that the tide is rising, and there is growing apprehension about the dangers which confront us. Some have suggested that we are threatened by a sort of barbarism not seen since the so-called Dark Ages. Even Hollywood movie-makers have appropriated the idea of society in decline for such movies as *RoboCop* and *The Terminator*.

What Has Happened?

The troubles that beset advanced industrial countries should serve to remind us how fragile—as well as rare—free societies are. Throughout human history, times of severe crisis (such as during a plague or civil war) have shown that human beings are apt to abandon all social and even self-restraint when conditions are dire enough. The celebrated Greek historian Thucydides wrote powerfully about the breakdown of civilized behavior in Athens during the terrible plague in 430 B.C., at the time of the Peloponnesian War. "Athens owed to the plague the beginnings of a state of unprecedented lawlessness.... People now began openly to venture on acts of self-indulgence which before then they used to keep dark. Thus they resolved to spend their money quickly and to spend it on pleasure, since money and life alike seemed equally ephemeral. As for what is called honour, no one showed himself willing to abide by its laws, so doubtful was it whether one would survive to enjoy the name for it."[5]

But the disappearance of self-restraint that can be seen all around us, especially in the culture of Hollywood and the arts, is striking and unprecedented because our society is not in crisis. Indeed, never have more Americans enjoyed more wealth and security. How has this come about? What are the sources of the breakdown—as yet small, but ominous—in societal norms and civilized behavior?

It has been suggested that one source of trouble in advanced industrial societies is found in the very nature of a capitalistic economy, which promotes consumerism and materialism because of the need to sell the products produced by an ever-growing economy. While there is per-

---

[5] Thucydides, *History of the Peloponnesian War*, translated by Rex Warner (London: Penguin, 1954), p. 155.

haps some truth to this thesis, one must ask why the problems appear just now, in the last third of the twentieth century, since capitalist economies and increasing prosperity are not new phenomena. Unless one believes that most people have all the products they want, it would seem that the continuing desire to improve their condition would promote hard work and self-restraint. It seems to me that a more plausible answer must be sought.

I believe that the real source of the difficulties that threaten our social fabric is something more fundamental, namely, an infection of relativism. This infection has both social and philosophical causes. On the one hand, relativism is an outgrowth of the egalitarian ethos that flourishes naturally, even inevitably, in liberal democracies such as the United States. Liberal democracy takes for granted that no individual is better than any other, and this seems to mean that the moral judgment or "value-calculus" of any person is worth as much as that of any other person. Carried to its logical conclusion, this egalitarianism undermines even parental authority. After all, who is to say that the judgment of a teacher or a father is superior to that of an eighteen-year-old, or for that matter a five-year-old? If the tendency toward relativism is inherent in liberal democracies, we should not be surprised that we see its effects only as time passes, since it takes generations for old habits of deference to authority to erode.

But relativism also has roots in certain philosophical

developments at the end of the last century. Some philosophers—most notably Friedrich Nietzsche—observed that all cultures live in terms of beliefs about what is highest or most desirable. Nietzsche asserted that these beliefs are the "values" of a culture. Using history, he argued, we can now see that no culture's values are more valid than those of any other. The conclusion from the philosopher's premises was stark: all values are equally "true" or valid, but also, from another culture's perspective, equally false. This means there is no basis for claims about right and wrong, or good and bad, outside of a particular culture. There is nothing good or bad for human beings by nature, and there are no permanent moral truths.

Today this philosophy is called "postmodernism," and in one way or another it has spread widely in our culture, especially in educational institutions. For more than two generations now, students from old-fashioned backgrounds have gone off to universities where they encounter these doctrines, returning home to disabuse their parents of the primitive conviction that there is a difference between right and wrong, or good and bad.

If there is no foundation for the distinction between good and bad conduct, then there is no basis for self-restraint. After all, in the name of what should one restrain oneself? Doesn't self-restraint depend on having some conception of what is right and what is wrong, so that we can learn to restrain low impulses for the sake of higher things? If higher and lower are merely individual "values," self-restraint loses its meaning. Here we come to the crux of the problem of our time, the problem described above as the collapse of belief in human nature. The view that what is good and bad for human beings is only a matter of mere "values" is identical to the view that *there is no human nature*. If there is no human nature, the idea of the best social order also loses its meaning.

Now, for nearly 2,500 years the greatest thinkers of the Western tradition—the writers whose ideas comprise this book—devoted themselves to the task of describing the best social order, based on a careful and unbiased investigation into human nature. This enterprise—which is called political philosophy—was regarded by the greatest thinkers, from Plato to Hegel, as the most important of all studies.

This book is my attempt at a serious yet accessible introduction to the great thinkers who planted the tree of liberty, a tree the fruits of which Americans, in particular, enjoy but take for granted. Without a doubt we live in a difficult season, and today some of those fruits fail to ripen, or when gathered, are bitter. But it is my conviction that the tree is still vital, and that we can preserve it for ourselves and our children by tending to it, by learning to cherish not only the fruits, but the roots of freedom.

After September 11, 2001

Most Americans who were alive on September 11, 2001, will never forget that terrible morning. The horrifying events of that day are said to have changed the world. Many of us feel that things are radically different now, but I believe it is not the world that has changed. The world remains precisely what it was before September 11, but our perception of the world—what we recognize to be true and what we consider important—has changed, and for the better. Before the attacks many Americans lived in what seems now to have been a make-believe world. They refused to acknowledge that there are evil people on our planet, that not everyone loves liberty, and that many people neither share in nor care about what we call civilization. September 11, 2001, marked the end of "a low, dishonest decade," as W. H. Auden once called another prewar period.

After the collapse of the Soviet Union, the United States no longer appeared to have enemies, and many Americans found it easy to ignore the ominous signs in other quarters that all was not well. The make-believe world into which we retreated was peaceful and prosperous (as indeed was most of the decade of the 1990s), and those living in it could or would not see the threats to freedom just over the horizon. It is reported, for example, that in a 1998 speech former President Clinton said that "the world is at peace and we have no enemies." The first

World Trade Center bombing (1993), the hasty with-
drawal of American soldiers from Mogadishu, Somalia,
after taking casualties in a firefight with a local warlord
(1993), the bombing of U.S. embassies in Kenya and
Tanzania (1998), the bomb attack on the USS Cole in
Yemen (2000)—most Americans saw these events as unre-
lated and somehow not very serious. But to others in the
world these events (and more importantly, the lack of a
serious U.S. response to them) formed a pattern and
taught a lesson: that the once vaunted United States of
America was not just feckless in her policies, but weak
militarily, lacking the resolve and courage to fight. We
know this now, of course, from the statements of Osama
bin Laden, one enemy of the U.S. who was interpreting
the signs.

The months following September 11 have been heart-
ening, and Mr. Bin Laden—if he is still alive—may be
reassessing the vitality of Western civilization, or at least of
that part of it he sent his minions to attack with hijacked
jetliners. It seems to me that the U.S. does not face any
new perils, but is now in a better position to recognize
and resist the dangers she has always faced even when pre-
tending they didn't exist. Islamofascism (or Islamism or
Wahhabism or whatever we call what bin Laden represents) shares quite a number of views with its counterparts
of the previous century, the fascisms and totalitarianisms
defeated in the great wars of the twentieth century

(including the Cold War). Each of these movements believed the West to be a cesspool of decadence, in contrast to its own moral purity. Each believed the United States to be not only soft, but timid and fearful, hiding behind weapons that can strike from a distance but unwilling to fight *mano a mano*. Even friends of the West or Western institutions (such as Aleksandr Solzhenitsyn, or Leo Strauss) spoke in the twentieth century of the "decline of the West," the "Crisis of European Rationalism," the "failure of nerve" of western societies. And although it is still too early to tell whether Americans have the resolve to carry on the war against terrorism, their initial reaction to the events of 9/11 provides some grounds for confidence that the direst warnings may have been overblown. God willing, we will overcome.

Chapter 1

ROOTS IN ANCIENT GREECE

Modern Western "democracies," as they are usually called, are actually better described as liberal commercial societies. They rest on principles of individualism and individual rights—especially legal rights—which are more fundamental than democracy, and also much newer. Democracy, after all, is an ancient Greek word for "rule by the many," and democracies have not until quite recently been regarded as very good or fair types of governments. The many can oppress the few quite as easily as the reverse, and the notion of individual rights actually has more to do with limiting the power of any government—whether by the many, or by a king, or by a party—to treat individuals unjustly.

In a very general way the core idea of liberal commercial societies is individualism. The view that has gained acceptance in the last three hundred years in the West is that society should be thought of as a collection of individuals whose needs and purposes lead them to constitute society, or to continue living in a society, as a way of furthering their individual needs and purposes. This individualism thus presumes that human beings should be understood primarily as individual organisms, who are what they are whether or not they live in some social order. More than that, it presumes that the needs and goals of human individuals—not just survival, but dignity, the active use of faculties, and a measure of security and comfort—are able to be understood in reference to individual men and women, with society but a means to achieve the goals or supply the needs more reliably or more easily.

This view of human beings as individuals "by nature" was advanced as a challenge to the view that rested at the core of classical political science, a mode of thinking which prevailed in the West (where it was invented in ancient Greece) for nearly two thousand years. The modern view can best be understood in comparison to the older view it replaced. The prevailing modern view was not unknown to ancient or classical thinkers, of course, but they rejected it in favor of an understanding more closely connected to their conception of the nature of all things.

The ancient Greek political philosophers taught that man is by nature a political being. By this they meant that human beings are suited naturally—by nature—for life in a particular sort of community, called a *polis* or city. Any human being not fortunate enough to live in a *polis,* they said, would not be capable of realizing his full humanity or "humanness."

They also knew that many, if not most, men and women were cut off from the possibility of being fully human because they lived either outside cities (as nomads or shepherds, condemned to what Marx later disparaged as the "idiocy of rural life"), or in vast empires, far too large to have any taste of genuine political life. The special characteristic of a city or *polis* is that in a city human beings are able to exercise one of their highest, most human faculties, which the Greeks called *logos* or reasoned speech. This capacity is involved in all political deliberation, by which human beings exercise *choice* about how to live and how to constitute social life itself. According to Aristotle, the faculty of *logos* distinguishes men from all other animals. It is also what makes man the only being who is political by nature. Any man who lives outside a *polis*, he taught, must be either a beast or a god—either less than human (because falling short of the true human potential) or more than human (and hence self-sufficient).

The Greeks thought one should conceive the nature of anything by thinking about its perfection or completion, that is, what the thing is able to be in the best or most appropriate circumstances. This is an extraordinarily dynamic way of looking at things: each particular example of a thing (whether a man or an oak tree), since it falls short of perfection, could be said to point beyond itself to what it ought to be. This exciting idea led men to think about what a *polis* or city ought to be, or what the nature of political life would be in its full perfection. And this is where complexities began to develop. The lofty idea that man is a political being by nature seemed, on reflection, to have troubling consequences in at least two respects.

One troubling implication was brought out by Aristotle himself, the greatest classical political scientist. He began by examining the claim that man's political nature is only fully developed when human beings live in a community and rule themselves, that is, when they speak, deliberate, and choose. If ruling is a noble and challenging occupation, one which develops and displays man's highest faculties, it would seem obvious that anyone seeking to develop his capacities and test himself to the fullest would seek to rule, and seek to rule in the most challenging circumstances. If this is so, then to rule a larger territory or more people—which is more difficult—must be better, and to rule on a larger scale would show a man to be more fully human than someone who rules a smaller city or fewer people. Thus the notion that political rule is the most human or noble calling seems to lead to the consequence that just as a man will seek to extend his rule, a fully developed *polis* will seek to rule over others. Such a *polis* will be, in short, imperialistic in its inclinations. For

Aristotle this logic suggested the need to reexamine the notion of political activity as choiceworthy for its own sake.

A second troubling consequence was harder for Aristotle to see, because it challenged the very notion that man is political by nature, an idea he accepted. But in the long run it was a more powerful objection, and played a decisive role in the modern rejection of the classical notion that man is political by nature. If man is political by nature, a man can only become fully human if he is fortunate enough to live in a political community, and indeed in one which permits or even encourages the full flowering of his most human capacities. If we understand human nature this way, we must conclude that *what* a human being becomes depends on the *polis* or city where that human being grows up. Thus he would be indebted to the city for his very humanness, for those capacities that set him apart as fully human. On such an understanding, a man's primary relation to the city or *polis* is one of obligation. The duties of citizenship, which can be very burdensome, would have the greatest claim on a man's time and attention because the individual is in principle subordinate to the *polis* or city.

But is there then any limit to what the city can ask of the citizens or subject them to? Does the city's claim on the citizen cover not merely his time and loyalty but his property? Does it extend even to his children? Must everything be understood as belonging in principle to the *polis* first? And what of those who are not rulers in the city—since not all can be rulers? Is there anything valuable in their lives? Are there any human capacities they can display or enjoy or take pride in? Doesn't the elevation of the political realm in such an understanding mean at the same time the denigration of all other human endeavors, of the other parts of human life?

In many ancient cities—even republics—the individual *was entirely* subordinate to the city. In ancient Sparta or early Rome, it was the citizen's duty—indeed crowning glory—to produce children for the republic's armies, and at the merest request of his authorities to sacrifice his own life for the city. And the most "political" of these communities, which understood men as political being, were indeed devoted largely to war and conquest, just as Aristotle suggested that they must or would be, based on the internal logic that exalted ruling and political life.

But if there were two troubling consequences to the lofty idea that man is a political being, there were also two suggestions for avoiding the troubling consequences. One was theoretical, the other practical. Aristotle's theoretical attempt to resolve the problem was based on the suggestion that while man is a political being by nature, he is also potentially more than that. The idea that political activity is the highest way of exercising the distinctly human virtues is, according to Aristotle, based on a mistaken understanding of "activity." It is agreed, he said, that "the best way of life both separately for each individual and in common for cities is that accompanied by virtue."[1] But while some believe virtue is displayed only in political life and ruling, others say another kind of activity exists which is *not* political, though it does involve the highest faculties. This other kind of active life involves the life of the mind, and points to the philosophic life as the highest or best, rather than that of political rule. But surely a city cannot be devoted to philosophy, the province of only a few rare and gifted minds? Aristotle's compromise between these two notions is to say that, while it is not possible for a city to lead the philosophic life, a sort of approximation to or echo of the philosophic life can be found in a life devoted to education and the arts. These, he said, are proper concerns for a city. The best possible city, then, would be one not devoted to ruling, war, and tyranny over others, but to the "internal activities" of education, drama, and the other arts.

Of course Aristotle never expected to see such a city. He was aware of the fragility and difficulty of sustaining even a decent city, let alone the best city one could imagine. Yet in the generation before Aristotle's birth, a city had existed which, in some respects, hinted at or anticipated

---

[1] Aristotle, *The Politics*, translated by Carnes Lord (Chicago: University of Chicago Press, 1984), 7.1, 1323b40–41. References are to the Bekker numbers.

his idea of the best city. Athens, the great *polis* which was finally to be defeated by the astonishing military prowess of Sparta, enjoyed in her greatest days a way of life that was self-consciously "balanced" in the way it viewed politics. Thucydides, the great historian of the war between Athens and Sparta (and himself an admirer of the regime of the Spartans) reported on a speech given by Pericles, the great Athenian leader. The speech is called the funeral oration of Pericles. Its words (perhaps composed by Thucydides) have been celebrated for more than two thousand years, because they offered, in tribute to the Athenians who had died in the war, a moving and impressive account of the Athenian way of life.

> Our constitution, is called a democracy because power is in the hands not of a minority but of the many. When it is a question of settling private disputes, everyone is equal before the law; when it is a question of putting one person before another in positions of public responsibility, what counts is not membership of a particular class, but the actual ability which the man possesses. No one, so long as he has it in him to be of service to that state, is kept in political obscurity because of poverty. And, just as our political life is free and open, so is our day-to-day life in our relations with each other. We do not get into a state with our next-door neighbour if he enjoys himself in his own way, nor do we give him the kind of black looks which, though they do no real harm, still do hurt people's

feelings. We are free and tolerant in our private lives; but in public affairs we keep to the law. This is because it commands our deep respect."[2]

Pericles drew an explicit contrast with Sparta with regard to the overwhelming emphasis placed by the Spartans on war, on defense and military training—all the things that required total subordination of the individual to the *polis* in Sparta. As Pericles put it, "there is a great difference between us and our opponents, in our attitude towards military security. Here are some examples: Our city is open to the world, and we have no periodical deportations in order to prevent people observing or finding our secrets which might be of military advantage to the enemy. This is because we rely, not on secret weapons, but on our own real courage and loyalty. There is a difference, too, in our educational systems. The Spartans, from their earliest boyhood, are submitted to the most laborious training in courage; we pass our lives without all these restrictions, and yet are just as ready to face the same dangers as they are."[3]

As these words suggest, the ancient Greeks were aware, however dimly, of the possibilities of individualism. For at least a brief time, in at least one ancient *polis*, men and

[2]Thucydides, *History of the Peloponnesian War*, translated by Rex Warner (London: Penguin, 1954), p. 145.
[3]*Ibid.*, p. 146.

women took seriously the idea that not everything should be subordinated to the requirements of the community—at least in normal times, when the city was at peace. While Athenian individualism was a far cry from the individualism of modern liberal societies, its brief existence and quick demise teach an important lesson about the fragility of any social order willing to emphasize or tolerate the idea that an individual has dignity in his own right and not merely as a cog in the larger machine of political life.

But individualism—notwithstanding its appearance in the ancient world, Christian as well as pagan—never attained prominence in that world. What we have glimpsed briefly in long-ago Athens soon disappeared, and many centuries were to pass before a genuine individualism was to appear again, on more solid foundations. In the following chapters we will explore those foundations. Our goal is to trace the development of this idea and of other key ideas about man, about nature, law, society, and the goals of life, which eventually allowed societies of free individuals to emerge. Such societies have existed for a very brief span, considered against the background of human history in general, and their existence may depend, more than most people think, on the ideas men and women hold dear.

Chapter 2

ROOTS IN
PREMODERN CHRISTIANITY

Before we move to the modern period, when the most important of the roots of free society begin to grow, it is worthwhile to glance briefly at the contributions of the ancient Christian understanding of man and the cosmos. It should be emphasized, however, that the ideas we will consider—as with those of the Greeks—are more properly seen as glimpses or anticipations of the principles that are the real bedrock of a free society.

There are four ways in which the early Christian understanding of man, and of man's place in "the scheme of things," offer us a glimpse of the foundations of freedom. At the time of Jesus, the distinctive feature of the ancient Mediterranean world was the enormous power and authority of Rome and the Roman Empire. Roman legions occupied vast portions of the known world and enforced what is called the Pax Romana, the peace and order under Roman imperial rule, backed up by the often ruthless use of arms. In this world, as in most of the ancient communities, the individual counted for nothing. The life of a particular man, woman, or child was of little value, because it was measured in relation to the importance of Rome itself, the Imperial City.

A story from Plutarch, related by the modern author Jean-Jacques Rousseau, tells us something important about the way the world was understood by people in ancient times. The story concerns a Spartan woman, and it brings out the attitude of genuine citizenship that was the goal of the ancient republics. The woman had five sons in the Spartan army, and she anxiously awaited news of the battle in which they fought. A messenger arrives, and, "trembling, she asks him for news. 'Your five sons were killed.' 'Base slave, did I ask you that?' 'We won the victory.' The mother runs to the temple and gives thanks to the gods. This is the female citizen," Rousseau tells us.[1] The lesson of the story is the insignificance of individuals—even loved ones, even five sons!—in relation to the city or political community.

What was true of the Greek city of Sparta was true also of Rome in her days of greatness as a republic. And under the terrible power of the Roman emperors, even though the grandeur of personal sacrifice had probably lost much

[1]Jean-Jacques Rousseau, *Emile, or On Education*, translated by Allan Bloom (New York: Basic Books, 1979), Book I, p. 40.

of its luster, the individual counted for even less. A particular individual was of no consequence when measured against the glory and stability of the empire. The imperial Pax Romana was a time of very little freedom. Yet it is just at this time that the life and teachings of Jesus, who was in human terms an insignificant carpenter from a backward province of the empire, offer us a glimpse of a very different understanding of things. He and his followers taught men and women to think of themselves—each one individually—as significant in the eyes of God. The dignity and even sanctity of every single human life, no matter how obscure, in the eyes of God, was one of the cardinal principles of the early Christians. And their God, in turn, was not the god of a city, or a tribe, or a nation, but the God of all human beings, and the savior of all individuals, of whatever tribe or nation, who were willing to turn their lives to His service. This universality, on the one hand, and emphasis on the individual, on the other, were hallmarks of Christianity from its earliest days, and the unusual combination of the two principles set Christianity apart from other ancient religions or religious sects. The Roman practice of adopting the gods of the nations they conquered, and giving them a place alongside their own Roman gods, worked nearly everywhere as a device for peaceful religious integration following conquest. But the God of the Jews and Christians did not fit the pattern of other ancient gods, and did not seem to fit into the Roman pantheon.

The distinctive Judeo-Christian conception of the divinity proved itself, in the long run, incompatible with the ancient tendency to subordinate the individual entirely to the state or empire.

A second contribution of Christianity involves the introduction of the idea of history, or of what is sometimes called "linear time." Does this mean ancient peoples before Christianity had no idea of history? Of course not. The earliest historian was in fact the Greek writer Thucydides, spoken of in the preceding chapter, author of *History of the Peloponnesian War*, which told the story of the epic war between Athens and Sparta. He is often called the father of history precisely because he attempted to write from a sci-entific or objective standpoint, that is, to write about the events of the war as a neutral observer, drawing on accounts supplied by eyewitnesses and checking them against other sources, and interpreting events without resort to supernatural forces or intervention of the gods as explanations. But Thucydides shared with his ancient pred-ecessors (whose chronicles of the stories of their peoples mixed fables and facts, and in whose accounts gods and men shared the stage) what we think of now as a cyclical view of history. They understood the passage of time in terms of the seasonal rhythms of the natural world, the endless succession of growth and decay, of coming into being and passing away, which mark the normal structure of all plant and animal (and human) life, as far as our senses are concerned. The famous words of Solomon, from the Hebrew Bible, capture this beautifully: "To everything… there is a season…."[2] Of course political empires, including the Eternal City, as Rome was known, were understood in the same terms, as subject to the cycle of life: birth, growth, and maturity, followed by decay and death.

Christianity brought something new to the understanding of history by teaching that God has entered into history and forever altered its cyclical nature. In the Christian conception, the history of man is itself a story with a beginning, and leading to an end—the day of judgment, the end of the world as human beings know it now. Why is this significant? Probably in the early days of Christianity it had little secular importance, since Christians were few and their apocalyptic views (many felt that the end of the world was imminent) meant that they had little influence. But with the passage of time—and the gradual erosion of the view that the world was about to end—a new implication of the idea of linear history began to take hold of men's minds: if history is not an endless cycle, if it is a story that shows that things change fundamentally in time, perhaps the change is progressive, perhaps over the course of human history there is *progress.* The notion of progress is itself a modern idea, but its roots can be discerned in the Christian doctrine that God enters historical time to save

[2]Ecclesiastes 3:1–8.

mankind. Progress means that man is not condemned to repeat the cycle of life endlessly, and this opens the possibility that man himself can improve his circumstances. We will see later how this leads in the beginning of the modern period to the secular idea of the transformation of the human condition itself.

A third contribution of Christianity to the roots of freedom is the principle (again, it flowers only in the modern period) of the separation of the realm of faith from the political realm. This is recognizable in Western societies today in many places, as the separation of church and state. Such a separation was unthinkable in the ancient world. In Egypt, in Athens, in Rome—in short, everywhere before the time of Christ—priests and rulers were closely connected. The Roman armies, for example, did not enter battle unless the auspices, as pronounced by sacred authorities, were favorable for victory. (The final and crushing Athenian defeat in Sicily, during the Peloponnesian War, was related to the refusal of Nicias, the Athenian commander, to rally his troops because he was awaiting a divine sign.) The connection between religion and rule is captured in the term "civil religion," which was the norm in the ancient world. The duties of citizenship were closely related to the obligations and observances of the city's religion, and citizens took it for granted that they should look to the sacred authorities for guidance in political affairs.

Jesus of Nazareth, however, taught his followers to look

at these matters in a new light. In the Christian view, the political realm is to be kept separate from the individual's relationship to God. When Jesus was asked by the Pharisees whether it is lawful to give tribute to Caesar, he showed them Caesar's image on a Roman coin, and answered that one should "render therefore unto Caesar the things which are Caesar's; and unto God the things that are God's."[3] The idea that political authorities do not have spiritual command of those under their civil jurisdiction is a necessary precondition for spiritual freedom. Although many centuries were to pass before the full implications of this doctrine were clear (during the Protestant Reformation; see chapter 5), the seeds of spiritual freedom can be located in this early Christian teaching. Eloquent testimony to the importance of this principle is found in the writings of twentieth-century political prisoners such as Aleksandr Solzhenitsyn, whose faith enabled him to survive many years of torture and suffering in the *gulag*—the prison camps of the communist regime of the former Soviet Union.

The fourth and final contribution of Christianity to the roots of freedom is the most difficult to explain, and admittedly is a principle that can be found in other ancient sources—most notably in the tradition of political philosophy, which began in Athens and whose founder was

[3]Matthew 22:15–21.

Socrates. But it seems appropriate to consider it a Christian contribution because in Christianity it became a popular notion, a notion that could spread to more than the few rare individuals who might be described as living philosophically. The principle is the conviction that there is such a thing as the truth, and that truth is accessible to human beings.

It is not uncommon today to encounter the idea that there is no truth. This idea might even be seen as a hallmark of our age, the late twentieth century or the age of "postmodernism." We will return to this subject in the final chapter. But although the view that there is no truth is at the core of postmodern philosophy (if that is not a contradiction in terms), it seems to have been "in the air" in many or most ages of human history. It expresses the cynical conviction that one can never really know anything, and that means, among other things, anything about what is right and wrong, or good and bad. This in turn fits nicely with the idea that, since we can never really know what is right or good, we may as well do whatever we want—that all of life is merely a struggle of one against another for whatever happens to seem desirable at the moment.

If this view is correct, there is no such thing as a just or proper foundation for political rule: whoever gets the power is by definition able to determine what is just or unjust, right or wrong. In this view, all of history is merely a struggle for power ("All history is the history of class struggles," as Marx and Engels expressed it in the *Communist Manifesto*). This, for example, is the basis of the postmodern feminist claim that Western history is the story of oppression of women by men, and that women should now seek to gain power in order to put an end to male oppression. They should do so, we are told, not because oppression is unjust (there is after all no justice) but because, since there is no alternative to power and the domination of some by others, a power struggle is inevitable, and women should seek to rule if they don't wish to be ruled.

The view that there is no truth was surely not unknown in the ancient world. It is captured nicely in the cynical words of Pontius Pilate, when he offered Jesus to his accusers to be crucified. In answer to Pilate's questions, Jesus had said that he had come into the world in order to "bear witness to the truth. Everyone that is of the truth heareth my voice." "What is truth?" the Roman official asked.[4]

How is truth connected to freedom? To reiterate: if there is no truth, there is no basis for right; all of life, including political life, is a struggle for power. But this means power is all that matters, and we can never be free. Even the one absolute ruler who holds power cannot escape the fact that his power has no foundation, and that others are constantly looking for a way to take this power and rule in their turn.

[4]John 18:37-38.

There is no escape from the endless quest for power, and no space, protected by walls of justice, where genuine freedom can be experienced. Only if there is truth, to which human minds have access—with or without divine assistance—can we discover a real possibility of liberty. It is no accident that Thomas Jefferson, in the manifesto known as the Declaration of Independence, speaks of the "truths" which we hold to be self-evident, in justifying the rebellion of the American colonies, carried out for the sake of political freedom. And although Greek philosophers beginning with Socrates had understood the implications of denying the existence of truth (Plato explored this theme in a dialogue called *Meno*), we must credit Christianity for spreading the idea beyond the circle of philosophers. The Gospel of John records Jesus's celebrated announcement to his followers— that if they are disciples indeed, "ye shall know the truth, and the truth shall make you free."[5]

Admittedly, Christianity is compatible with free society in other ways, as are other religions—if not the civil religions of antiquity. It must also be said that the Christian Church has not always, in practice, been friendly to the conditions of free society. It is obvious that powerful religious convictions can lead men to suppress liberty as well as to foster it. One might point to the rigors of the Inquisition in the late middle ages, or to the pogroms

[5]John 8:32.

against Jews, and milder forms of persecution and exclusion, which disfigured Europe over the course of many centuries.

But if one is looking at historical practice (as opposed to theory or the realm of ideas, as we have here), there is at least one more contribution of the Christian church to the roots of free society. As we will see in the next chapter, the church played an important though unintentional role in the complicated process by which modern liberty emerged out of feudalism. In the twelfth and thirteenth centuries, the church hierarchy in Western Europe was the first to seize on the practice of law after the recovery (or rediscovery) of a code of Roman law called the Pandects of Justinian, in Amalfi, Italy, in A.D. 1130. The leaders of the church were quick to realize that the law offered them an important way to preserve the church's extensive property, which was during the lawless feudal period vulnerable to predations of force. Thus the church found it to be in its worldly interest to encourage the spread of the rule of law, and to see that its own scholars were preeminent in the learning and practice of the law.

But this was an unintended effect of the church's position in medieval life, and was not directly connected to any of the church's doctrines. In the most important respects, as we have seen, its contribution consists in the introduction of the seeds of certain ideas—the separation of civil and spiritual authority, or the idea of linear history, making possible an idea of progress—which did not flower into genuine contributions to free societies for many centuries; in fact, not until the modern period, which began around 1500. Before turning to modernity itself, we make one more excursion into the premodern period to consider the emergence from feudalism.

Chapter 3

THE EMERGENCE
FROM FEUDALISM

In the second chapter we considered the idea of individualism itself, and traced its brief appearance in ancient Athens, where it flourished during the time of Pericles, from about 450 to 430 B.C., before Athens was conquered (in 404 B.C.) by neighboring Sparta, whose "armed camp" mentality proved to be too powerful for the Athenians to defeat in war. We turn now to a set of ideas related to an historical development of incalculable importance, namely, the emergence from feudalism. This development took several centuries, but it is one of the most distinctive features of the history of Western Europe, and Western Europe is where all the ideas and institutions of liberal society first appeared in the seventeenth and eighteenth centuries. Notions such as constitutional and limited government, separation of powers, government by consent, and representative democracy—which will be considered

in later chapters—all emerged in the nations of Western
Europe in connection with the ideas of philosophers such
as Thomas Hobbes, John Locke, and Charles Secondat,
Baron Montesquieu. But none of their ideas would have
been imaginable under the rigid order of feudalism,
which was the dominant mode of social organization well
into the sixteenth century, and was not substantially dissolved until the seventeenth century in England, and later
in France and other countries.

One of the greatest philosophers of recent centuries
was an eighteenth-century Scotsman named David
Hume. Hume was also an historian, and author of a six-
volume *History of England*.[1] Two of the volumes of Hume's
History deal extensively with the period during which the
feudal system first held sway and then was gradually dissolved. Hume thought deeply about the ideas and practices that brought the feudal order into being in the first
place and that later led to its dissolution. The circumstances that seem to call forth feudal arrangements are
more common—even in the world today—than one
would first think, and Hume teaches us to reflect on what
those circumstances tell us about human beings and the
social order.

---

[1] The *History of England* went through editions numbering well into the hundreds; there was no standard edition until the Liberty Fund Press (Indianapolis:
Liberty Classics) published theirs in 1983. Cited as *H* followed by volume and
page number.

The feudal system came into being when the ancient Roman Empire broke up and decayed after the death of Charlemagne. With their armies and bureaucratic system, the Romans had established a civil order in the lands of Europe, but as their order crumbled a kind of anarchy or chaos ensued. In this lawless and chaotic condition nothing was secure; danger, insecurity, poverty, and want were pervasive. The feudal order or feudal system grew up in response to these conditions, and though its features varied from place to place, enough similarities emerged to allow us to see a common organizational principle.

The main principle was quite simple: the social organization was strictly hierarchical, and almost nothing was permitted to exist outside the hierarchy. Though dressed in fancy terminology and dignified by a kind of theological sanction, the feudal system amounted to little more than a gigantic "protection racket," as it would be called today. All authority flowed in principle from a central authority figure, and all land or property belonged in principle to him. A holding, or a "place," could only be obtained by swearing fealty to someone above you in the hierarchy, and even then your place was contingent on continuous loyalty and service to the nominal "protector." Thus all lands belonged to the king, who granted "title" to some portion of land to a baron, in exchange for his promise of loyalty—and most important—his military service to the king. The baron, in turn, raised what

amounted to the officer corps of a private army, by granting smaller fiefs to members of the next rank of nobility
below him, in exchange for their promise to fight on his
behalf and at his command. This pattern prevailed at all
levels of the nobility, down to the seigneur or "holder" of
a simple farm, or manor. Below the rank of seigneur were
the laborers: villeins and serfs. Even serfs were permitted
to labor and raise crops only in exchange for the material
support they agreed to supply to the lord whose protection they received in return. This system—or something
similar—can still be seen in some parts of the less developed world, where private armies are the basis of what
order exists, personal loyalty is the cardinal principle of
private armies, and the rule of law is largely unknown.

Such a system has as its *raison d' être* the plain and obvious need for some kind of security from the predations of
roving bands of brigands. In exchange for security of this
very rudimentary sort, most people were willing to give
up their independence and swear loyalty, or fealty, to
someone who would offer protection. Property, under the
feudal system, was not really owned, because it could be
reclaimed by the holder of a fief with a higher rank. The
crucial feature of the system was that all the "functions" of
civil society were in the hands of the military chieftain,
who settled all disputes or complaints among those whose
loyalty he commanded. Everything was in principle subordinated to the military requirements of survival. It was

as if the military leader were also the police chief, and even more: he was also prosecutor, judge, and court of appeals.

In this condition, as Hume reported, men may appear to have complete liberty because there are no rules, but in fact they enjoy no genuine practical liberty. "Such a state of society was very little advanced beyond the rude state of nature."[2] The subordination of everything to considerations of security meant in practice a life scarcely better than that of animals in the forest. In such a desperate condition of anarchy there is no genuine liberty even though men appear to have complete liberty. "The reason is derived from the excess itself of that liberty," Hume went on. "Men must guard themselves at any price against insults and injuries; and where they receive no protection from the laws and magistrate, they will seek it by submission to superiors, and by herding in some inferior confederacy, which acts under the direction of a powerful chieftain. And thus all anarchy is the immediate cause of tyranny, if not over the state, at least over many of the individuals."[3]

And this is not the only effect of the feudal system. The "precarious state of feudal property," we learn from Hume, meant that "industry of no kind could have place

[2] *H* II:521.
[3] *H* I:169.

in the kingdom."[4] When the fruits of a man's industry or work are not secure to him, nearly every man will choose not to apply himself with energy and attention. Why clear land for farming if, once the land has become more valuable, it will be taken back by the superior at whose pleasure you hold the land in the first place? Agriculture, trade, and commerce will not develop in this condition. This state of affairs continues in many parts of the world today where property is not secure. As Hume expressed it, "the languishing state of commerce kept the inhabitants poor and contemptible; and the political institutions were calculated to render that poverty perpetual. The barons and gentry, living in rustic plenty and hospitality, gave no encouragement to the arts, and had no demand for any of the more elaborate produce of manufactures: every profession was held in contempt but that of arms. And if any merchant or manufacture rose by industry and frugality to a degree of opulence, he found himself but the more exposed to injuries, from the envy and avidity of the military nobles."[5] What is worse, once such a situation prevails there seems to be no escape from the vicious cycle of sloth and poverty.

What, then, can explain the dissolution of the feudal order? Hume located the key in a remote event of apparently minor importance. In England some special circum-

[4] *H* I:484.
[5] *H* I:463–64.

stances, including the Norman Conquest in particular, had already given a bit of help to the lower orders of society, because the conquering king and his descendants were inclined to suppress the powers of the barons more strictly in the conquered country than elsewhere. "But perhaps there was no event," Hume wrote, "which tended further to the improvement of the age, than one, which has not been much remarked, the accidental finding of a copy of Justinian's Pandects, about the year 1130, in the town of Amalfi in Italy."[6] Why was this so important? What were Justinian's Pandects?

The Pandects of Justinian was a code of Roman law, and the rule of law had long been missing in these barbarous ages. But when combined with certain other things, it would prove to be the means of escape from the vicious cycle of feudal poverty and insecurity. Within the space of ten years, Hume reports, lectures in the newly discovered civil law were being delivered by ecclesiastics at the University of Oxford. "That order of men, having large possessions to defend, were in a manner necessitated to turn their studies towards the law and their properties being often endangered by the violence of the princes and barons, it became their interest to enforce the observance of general and equitable rules, from which alone they could receive protection."[7]

[6] *H* II: 520.
[7] *Ibid.*

The code of laws was less important in itself than as a
kind of trigger that released tendencies which are inherent in human nature, but which remained hidden so long
as men lived in the radical insecurity of feudal depend-
ency. Where lands are first distributed as a kind of reward
for service in conquest, and held only on condition of
continued military service, there cannot be a fixed notion
of property. But where lands are cultivated, a kind of natural logic intrudes itself. "The attachment naturally
formed with a fixed portion of land, gradually begets the
idea of something like property, and makes the possessor
forget his dependant situation.... It seemed equitable, that
one who had cultivated and sowed a field, should reap the
harvest." The result was that fief holdings "at first entirely
precarious, were soon made annual."[8]

But as the rule of law replaced the whim of a military
master, further changes came naturally. At first the villeins
were virtual agricultural slaves to the "military posture" of
the chieftain, whose readiness had to be constantly maintained. They were occupied "entirely in the cultivation of
their master's land, and paid their rents either in corn or
cattle and other produce of the farm, or in servile
offices.... In proportion as agriculture improved, and
money encreased, it was found, that these services, tho'
extremely burthensome to the villein, were of little

[8] *H* I:458.

advantage to the master; and that the produce of a large estate could be much more conveniently disposed of by the peasant himself, who raised it, than by the landlord or his bailiff, who were formerly accustomed to receive it."[9] The result was the introduction of the more convenient practice of paying rent instead of services, and later indeed of money rents rather than those "in kind," that is, in corn or wheat. "And as men, in a subsequent age, discovered, that farms were better cultivated where the farmer enjoyed a security of possession, the practice of granting leases to the peasant began to prevail, which entirely broke the bonds of servitude, already much relaxed from the former practices."[10] The system of villenage, Hume notes, thus "went gradually into disuse throughout the more civilized parts of Europe: The interest of the master, as well as that of the slave, concurred in this alteration."[11] And as the distinction between freeman and villein disappeared, the political aspect of modern Europe began to take shape. "Thus *personal* freedom became almost general in Europe; an advantage which paved the way for the encrease of *political* or *civil* liberty."[12]

How can the same reasoning concerning the convenience of property ownership and inheritance explain both

[9] *H* II:523.

[10] *H* II:524.

[11] *Ibid.*

[12] *Ibid.*

the formation and dissolution of the feudal land tenure system? The crucial factor, according to Hume, has already been noted: the development of the rule of law following the recovery of the Pandects of Justinian. During the ages when the feudal system was solidifying, Hume points out repeatedly, military concerns were paramount because there was no effective law. Indeed the "judiciary" itself, such as it was, was constituted largely by the military chieftains; as is "unavoidable to all nations that have made slender advances in refinement," these men "everywhere united the civil jurisdiction with the military power."[13] "Law, in its commencement, was not an intricate science, and was more governed by maxims of equity, which seem obvious to common sense, than by numerous and subtle principles, applied to a variety of cases by profound reasonings from analogy. An officer, tho' he had passed his life in the field, was able to determine all legal controversies which could occur within the district committed to his charge; and his decisions were the most likely to meet with a prompt and ready obedience, from men who respected his person, and were accustomed to act under his command."[14]

Since judicial authority was combined with military command and both were attached to an hereditary fief

[13] *H* I:459-60.
[14] *H* I:460.

holding, they were, as a unit, transmitted by inheritance. The feudal lords were able, said Hume, to "render their dignity perpetual and hereditary. . . .After this manner, the vast fabric of feudal subordination became quite solid and comprehensive."[15] The tendencies that acted to solidify this system operated as long as law and justice were virtually identical to the chieftain's word, and this was the natural condition where military considerations were paramount, where "men, not protected by law in their lives and properties, sought shelter, by their personal servility and attachments, under some powerful chieftain; or by voluntary combinations."[16]

But as the science of law spread, those who knew it became more important, and the development of this special skill meant that the functions of judge and military leader no longer were performed by the same man. Rather there appeared the beginnings of what we call an "independent judiciary"—officials who apply "known and settled *laws*," which are the principles and practices that have evolved over a long period. Thus we find three ideas of central importance in the disintegration of the feudal order: the rule of law, the idea of judges *independent* of military chieftains (independent judiciary), and the idea of property ownership rather than "holdings" secured by

---

[15] *Ibid.*

[16] *H* II:521-22.

personal loyalty. As we will see in later chapters, property ownership by individuals ("private property"), the rule of law, and an independent judiciary are key features of all liberal commercial societies, though it took several centuries for these ideas to develop to their "modern" form. We will see how important their role is especially when we consider the ideas of John Locke, the famous seventeenth-century English political philosopher.

Chapter 4

THE PROTESTANT REFORMATION

In the last chapter we traced the gradual development of three ideas that are indispensable components of the bedrock of liberal society, ideas that grew up as practices in the centuries when feudalism began to dissolve in what is now Western Europe: ownership of private property, the rule of law, and an independent judiciary. Here we look at another historical—as opposed to philosophical—development, one that also changed the face of Western Europe: the Protestant Reformation.

The Reformation is perhaps the single most important development that separates the experience of the peoples of northwestern Europe from the experience of the other European peoples with whom in other respects they share a heritage. All of Europe shares roots in ancient Greece and Rome and in the Judeo-Christian tradition. But the Protestant Reformation was a distinctly northwest

European phenomenon. And it is no accident that the chief ideas and institutions of modern liberal commercial society appeared in northwestern Europe, among the very nations and peoples that experienced the Protestant Reformation firsthand, above all in Britain, the Low Countries, France, and Germany. Why this should be so is an interesting question. We will see that the Reformation exerted its influence on the formation of liberal commercial society in two quite different ways, one positive and one, so to speak, negative. In the second sense, in fact, the Reformation could be described as having generated a crisis to which the institutions of liberal society were a response and solution.

In the late Middle Ages Christianity was of course the reigning creed in the nations of Europe, north as well as south, and from Spain and France in the west to the Russian empire in the east. And by Christian is meant Catholic, whether Eastern or Roman Catholic. The doctrines of the various Christian churches were everywhere in Europe regarded as authoritative. Our focus is on Western Europe, where the Roman Catholic pope wielded enormous power. Kings and princes were believed to rule by divine authority as God's vice-regents on earth, and in spiritual matters particularly were expected to listen to Rome.

As often happens with powerful and entrenched bureaucracies, however, the Roman Catholic Church by the fifteenth century had become in many ways corrupt: some popes were widely known to have behaved in ways unbecoming to sacred authorities, sometimes even using the powers of their office to further the careers of their illegitimate children. The widespread sale of papal indulgences was becoming a scandal. Already possessing enormous wealth, the Church accumulated more by a kind of extortion. Simple folk were persuaded to buy indulgences from the Church to help their deceased loved ones escape from purgatory, over which the religious authorities claimed to exercise an influence. But aside from the sale of indulgences, the Church also claimed an absolute authority in all things sacred. The very meaning of sacred texts was a matter for hierarchical Church authorities to determine, and laymen not only were discouraged from reading the scriptures, but generally did not even have access to them. This was in part because the sacred texts were available only in Latin, the language of the educated class, but even churchmen who were learned in Latin were obliged to defer to higher authorities in determining the meaning of the religious texts.

The Protestant Reformation was a reaction against the Roman Catholic Church's power in two chief ways, one mainly doctrinal and one political, though often these are difficult to separate. The doctrinal revolution has its roots primarily in the writings and teachings of an early sixteen-century German monk, Martin Luther, an

Augustinian and doctor of theology who began to challenge the practices—and doctrines—of the Roman Catholic Church. The beginning of the Reformation is often dated at 1517 when Luther nailed his "Ninety-Five Theses" to the church door at Wittenberg, where he was a professor. The theses attacked the practice of selling papal indulgences. In the years that followed Luther was engaged in a series of controversies with papal authorities, was placed under a papal ban, and finally excommunicated when he refused to renounce his writings.

But the age was ripe for Luther's challenge, and he was supported in many cases by the local rulers—princes in the districts of Germany and northern Europe who were happy to see the iron rule of the Roman Catholic Church hierarchy challenged at its foundations. Without Luther even knowing it, the "Ninety-Five Theses" were surreptitiously translated from Latin into German and widely circulated in the German countryside. The recent invention of the printing press was only one of the many factors contributing to the force and effectiveness of Luther's revolutionary challenge. A few years later, when confined for his protection in the Wartburg Castle, Luther began a translation of the Bible into German, the language of ordinary people. This enormously important project made the Scriptures available to lay people for the first time.

The political side of the Protestant Reformation can be seen most clearly across the English channel, though politics of course played some part in Luther's revolution as well. King Henry VIII of England, after chafing under the pope's authority for nearly thirty years of his reign, and wishing to divorce his wife, which the pope would not condone, seized the initiative in 1538, by declaring the church in Britain—and himself as head of it—independent of the long reach of Rome. Perhaps most important, he disbanded the monasteries, seizing huge quantities of the Roman Catholic Church's wealth. Ruins of the monasteries abandoned four and a half centuries ago can still be seen in Britain today.

But whether we look at the political or theological side of the Reformation, in the most fundamental sense, it was a reaction against central authority, especially distant authority, in the name of individual judgment (Luther) or local rule (Henry VIII of England). The nature of Luther's theological revolution is not our concern here, except insofar as it contributed to the ideas that in succeeding centuries became the basis of liberal societies. And it plainly did contribute. Luther emphasized the importance of the individual and the direct relation between the individual and God, thus undermining the role claimed by the Roman Catholic hierarchy, which had, since the beginnings of Christianity, interpreted Scripture, absolved sins, and so on. According to Luther, only God can forgive our sins, not a priest, and each person must confront God as an individual, convinced in his faith that God's righteousness is mercy. According to Luther, salvation depends on faith, not on works, and thus no "certificate of indulgence" purchased with worldly wealth could play any role in the true Christian's salvation. The demotion this entailed for all the ranks of Roman Catholic clergy is nicely captured in the Lutheran phrase the "priesthood of all believers." All the Protestant denominations, including those that grew up around Luther's contemporaries such as John Zwingli, emphasized the importance of the individual and the individual's responsibility to read and interpret the Scriptures on his own.

The political ramifications of this revolution were of course not lost on Luther or his contemporaries. Although it took several hundred years to work out what we might call the secular revolution that occurred at the same time as the Protestant one, there is a striking parallel between the political doctrines—such as individualism and government by consent—and their theological counterparts. For the sake of convenience, we will mention three aspects here.

First and perhaps most important is the very split just now mentioned, namely, the division between the temporal and spiritual realms. This was, of course, not a new theme for Christians (Christ had taught them to "render unto Caesar the things that are Caesar's"), but the overwhelming power of the Roman Catholic hierarchy in the late Middle Ages had tended to confuse the two realms, and the Church rulers often exercised temporal as well as spiritual authority. Luther wrote with bitterness: "My ungracious lords, the pope and the bishops, should be bishops and preach God's Word; this they leave undone and are become temporal princes, and govern with laws which concern only life and property. How thoroughly they have turned things upside down."[1] "Inwardly they ought to be ruling souls by God's Word; but outwardly they rule castles, cities, land and people and torture souls with unspeakable outrages."[2] Thus, according to Luther, the spiritual realm should be distinct from secular or worldly concerns, and he blamed the Roman Catholic Church for confusing them. If all men were true Christians, Luther admitted, no temporal government would be needed: in his own words, "it is indeed true that Christians, so far as they themselves are concerned, are subject to neither law nor sword and need neither; but first take heed and fill the world with real Christians before ruling it in a Christian and evangelical manner." However, he continued, "this you will never accomplish."[3] Even when all are baptized and "nominally Christian," Luther wrote, "few believe and still fewer live a Christian life."[4]

---

[1] Martin Luther, "Secular Authority: To What Extent It Should Be Obeyed," translated by J. J. Schindel and reprinted in *Martin Luther: Selections*, edited by John Dillenberger (New York: Anchor Books, 1961), p. 386.

[2] *Ibid*.

[3] *Ibid*., p. 371.

[4] *Ibid*., p. 370.

Temporal laws are necessary, he continued, because without them, "seeing that the whole world is evil and that among thousands there is scarcely one true Christian, men would devour one another, and no one could preserve wife and child, support himself and serve God; and thus the world would be reduced to chaos."[5] This is why, according to Luther, "God has ordained the two governments," the spiritual and the secular. As we will see in a later chapter, this principle became absolutely central in modern liberal societies, where—as Locke taught nearly two centuries later in his famous *Letter Concerning Toleration*—the civil authorities have no responsibility for men's souls and should not attempt to control their minds. As Luther put it in 1523, "worldly government has laws which extend no farther than to life and property and what is external upon earth. For over the soul God can and will let no one rule but Himself. Therefore, where temporal power presumes to prescribe laws for the soul, it encroaches upon God's government and only misleads and destroys the souls."[6]

A second political ramification of Luther's revolution involves the idea of individual responsibility, another cardinal principle in liberal societies. The Roman Catholic Church expected complete submission from individuals in matters of scriptural interpretation. Thus any attempt to

[5] *Ibid.*

[6] *Ibid.*, pp. 382-83.

understand the Bible was subject to review by Church authorities, and in fact, ordinary people—perhaps not able to read at all and certainly not able to read Latin—had no access to the holy Scriptures except through their priests. Luther was himself censured by the pope for interpreting the Bible without the approval of the Church fathers. But Luther overturned this state of things. He translated the Bible into the vernacular so that Scriptures could be understood (if not read) by the common people. He also insisted that every individual is responsible for confronting the Christian teaching on his own. "Every man is responsible for his own faith," Luther wrote, "and he must see to it for himself that he believes rightly. As little as another can go to hell or heaven for me, so little can he believe or disbelieve for me; and as little as he can open or shut heaven or hell for me, so little can he drive me to faith or unbelief."[7] Faith is a matter of individual concern and responsibility. The Church in many cases did not permit the reading of the Bible by individuals in their homes (this practice was still being resisted by English Puritans in 1650!). Luther's powerful expression of resistance still resonates: "If you command me to believe, and to put away books, I will not obey; for in this case you are a tyrant and overreach yourself, and command where you have neither right nor power."[8] Individual conscience and individual

[7] *Ibid.*, p. 385.
[8] *Ibid.*, p. 388.

responsibility thus played vital roles in the Protestant Reformation.

The third idea that had political effects is connected to the first two and concerns the assertion—by Luther and other leaders of the Reformation—of the dignity and importance of the common man. We can hear, in these early writings, the first articulation of the idea known in liberal societies as "government by consent." There is even a democratic hint in these passages: "What, then, are the priests and bishops? I answer, Their government is not one of authority or power, but a service and an office; for they are neither higher nor better than other Christians. Therefore they should not impose any law or decree on others without their will and consent."[9] Moreover, Luther's prose rings with the notion that times are chang-ing, that, as he puts it, "the common man is learning to think." In fact he even seems to threaten civil disorder: "the prince's scourge, which God calls *contemptum*, is gath-ering force among the mob and with the common man. I fear there is no way to stop it, unless the princes conduct themselves in a princely manner and begin again to rule reasonably and thoroughly. Men ought not, men cannot, men will not suffer your tyranny and presumption much longer."[10]

[9] *Ibid.*, p. 392.
[10] *Ibid.*, p. 391.

It is important to add that Luther himself was no political revolutionary; he counseled the German peasants to submit to the often harsh rule of their feudal masters. But in the long run the revolution against hierarchy and authority, formulated in theological terms by Luther, could not help spreading into the political realm. It is probably no accident that a more clearly political notion—such as the claim that the basis of any civil order is a social contract among free and equal individuals—grew up in the same geographic areas where the Protestant Reformation took deepest root.

But there is another side to this story. Despite all the individual tenets of modern liberal society that were buried in the Protestant Reformation, like time-bombs waiting to explode later, the movement itself had a more immediate—and opposite—effect. This is because the Reformation resulted in religious wars. By the end of the century of the Reformation—by 1600, in other words—the battle lines were drawn. Within two decades northern Europe was thrown into religious convulsions. The Thirty Years War that tore apart France and the Low Countries from 1618 to 1648 was in the fundamental sense a religious war pitting Roman Catholics against Protestants.

One of the most significant by-products of this Catholic-Protestant conflict was the emigration to the "New World"—the Americas and particularly North America—of significant numbers of Protestants seeking the liberty to practice their version of Christian faith. In many of these early Protestant communities we can discover fundamental liberal principles—the social contract, individual responsibility, even in some cases the separation of secular and spiritual realms. But their very existence was the result of intolerance, and in some cases there were frictions between settlements practicing different forms of the Protestant faith; that is, as the settlers continued to practice against others the religious intolerance from which they themselves had fled.

In fact some of these Puritan communities in the New World were fanatical in their insistence on orthodoxy, and in some cases, the members were expected to sacrifice all individual liberty to a communitarian supervision that was virtually totalitarian, extending to all manner of personal behavior, dress, and speech. Thus we can say that the force of the Protestant Reformation worked in two ways: on the one hand, it spread the notions of individual responsibility and autonomy, and revolt against hierarchical authority, but on the other hand, it led to violent religious strife and in some cases astonishingly repressive communities, in which all individuality was given up, not to a hierarchy, but to a community "way of life"—often a democratic one. A later chapter deals with the distinction between democracies—which are consistent with a complete lack of individual liberty—and liberal individualist societies grounded in individual rights. For the moment it is enough to say that it was precisely these two by-products of the Reformation—religious wars and Puritan totalitarianism—that set the stage for perhaps the most important philosophers in the liberal tradition, Thomas Hobbes and John Locke, the two who more than any others articulated the fundamental principles of liberal individualist society.

Chapter 5

THE MODERN PROJECT

The two previous chapters traced the earliest origins of the modern notions of property, the rule of law, and an independent judiciary, in the emergence from feudalism in Britain and the Low Countries, and located the earliest glimmer of notions of individual conscience, separation of church and state, and government by consent in the Protestant Reformation. We turn now to the purely philosophical side of the modern revolution, which established the distinctly modern understandings of man, of nature, and of the purpose of political life itself.

Europe emerged from the Dark Ages over a period of several centuries. Such intellectual life as there was during those centuries was spurred on greatly by the recovery—to the West—of the writings of Aristotle, the great Athenian philosopher of 350 B.C., whose writings had been pre- served for many centuries by Islamic philosophers. In the

thirteenth century A.D., the Dominican Thomas Aquinas at
the University of Paris devoted his amazing career to a
synthesis of Christian theology and Aristotelian ethics and
natural philosophy, and won approval from the Roman
Catholic Church for the pagan thinker's political and
moral treatises. In the following centuries this philosophy
of "scholasticism," which used the concepts of Aristotle to
express theological and political theories, came to domi-
nate the medieval universities almost completely. As late as
the early seventeenth century in Britain, Thomas Hobbes
was to complain that his education at Oxford was filled
chiefly with "darkness from vain philosophy"[1] of scholasticism. These late medieval political theories have more in
common with the ideas of the pagan philosophers Plato
and Aristotle than with anything recognizably modern,
not to say liberal. The ideas of modern liberal society
required nothing less than an intellectual revolution of the
greatest magnitude.

Consider just one example of the persistent importance
of the ancient thinkers' views on politics and man. Sir
Thomas More, like his friend the great Dutch humanist
Erasmus, wrote treatises on politics during the first quarter
of the sixteenth century. His most renowned work, called
Utopia, was published in 1516. In *Utopia* More sketched the

---

[1]Thomas Hobbes, *Leviathan* (Indianapolis: Hackett Publishing Co., 1994), p.
453.

outline of an ideal commonwealth, in the tradition of Plato's *Republic*, which in fact it complemented in a sense by focusing on a side of the human soul which Plato had ignored in his treatise. The society of *Utopia*—most famous for its communism, its devotion to pleasure, and the nature of its people—"easy-going, good-tempered, ingenious, and leisure-loving"[2] is in fact wholly in the tradition of the political works of antiquity, and is replete with references to the ancient political philosophers whom More loved and studied deeply. Plato, Aristotle, Seneca, Cicero, Sallust, and Plutarch dot its pages.

But at the same time More was composing *Utopia*, an intellectual revolution was brewing in the mind of another great writer. The intellectual revolution of modernity has roots in many thinkers, but in none so much as the great Florentine statesman and political philosopher Niccolo Machiavelli, whose works date from the first decades of the sixteenthcentury, exactly the same time Sir Thomas More was writing his *Utopia*. Machiavelli's *The Prince*, written in 1513 but not published until after the author's death in 1526, is a tiny bombshell of a book, for it contains in scarcely one hundred pages almost all the principles of the revolutionary view of man, of political life, and of nature, which challenged directly

---

[2]St. Thomas More, *Utopia* (New Haven, Conn.: Yale University Press, 1964), Book II, p. 103.

and explicitly the views that had held sway in one form
or another for nearly two thousand years, wherever
Western thinkers reflected on man, morals, and politics.

How did Machiavelli offer his challenge, and what
principles did he advance to replace the old understanding? First we must summarize the old understanding, the
classical view of human nature and the purpose of political life, as it appears in the writings of the great classical
philosophers, above all in Plato and Aristotle. They taught
that man is by nature a *political* being, which means man
is a being who is intended by nature to live in a *polis*, a city
or a political community. The nature of anything, according to Aristotle, is seen only when one looks at the full
development of that thing—the essence of a thing is
revealed in its most perfect situation. Survival, then, as a
condition for pursuing the life of politics, where free
choice about a way of life can be exercised. Thus survival
is important, but only as a means to a higher end. We fight
wars in order to have peace and leisure, because only in
conditions of peace and leisure can human beings be fully
human. Aristotle therefore taught that the most important
questions for political philosophy are questions about
ends: How should we live once the conditions are secured
for a full human life? In war, or dire necessity, no questions
about ends or goals arise because one can only worry
about survival itself. This is what classical or ancient philosophy taught.

Machiavelli believed that the classical view was idealistic, that Plato and Aristotle had not understood what man
really is. He insisted on lowering the goals of political life
because, as he suggested in *The Prince*, most people are
concerned only with the security, comfort, and well-being
of themselves and their families. Most people pay no
attention to political life or to virtue as ends in themselves. And for most men, not public but private life is
what matters. This, Machiavelli suggests, is because what
the ancient philosophers believed were the peaceful and
stable conditions necessary for thinking about higher
goals never really exist anywhere: we are always in a state
of war—if only potentially—and we should remember
this even when times appear peaceful. According to
Machiavelli, the idealism of Plato and Aristotle is nowhere
so clearly expressed as in their belief that the true nature
of anything can be seen only in the best conditions. They
thought, for example, that a tree can only be seen as what
it truly "is"—what nature intends it to be—if it grows in
the best soil, with the best weather and no disturbing conditions. And human beings can only be fully human when
they have peace, plenty, and a stable political community.
Machiavelli challenged this way of understanding things at
its very foundation: we see what something *really* is, he
taught, only in the *worst* conditions, because that is when
all the decorations, the nonessential things, are stripped
away. Thus political life is best understood by reference to

war, not peace. Peace is only an illusion—a name for those brief times when the fundamental reality is temporarily covered over by misleading appearances. Anyone who takes his bearings from the best rather than the worst case will not survive long, because he will be easy prey for the man (or the nation) that sees through appearances to the fundamental reality. For human communities the fundamental reality is war and the struggle to survive.

Machiavelli sought—on the basis of this new way of looking at things—to introduce a new political science, a new understanding of man and of nature. The first two principles of this new approach we have already seen: 1) Things must be understood at their most basic, stripped of the mere appearances that decorate or hide them in ordinary experience. 2) The notion that the important questions are about ends or goals—such as what should we seek when we have the peace and leisure to choose—is silly because there is never peace and leisure in that sense: the fundamental reality of the human condition is war and struggle, even when it doesn't appear that way. (Appearances deceive, and we must be ruthless and realistic when we try to understand ourselves or other men.)

But these principles have implications far beyond what we see at first glance. The old humanistic political science, for example, taught that since wealth and money are only means to higher things—beauty, leisure, and the arts, for example—men should be educated to understand the low ranking of material things and to concern themselves with higher things. Aristotle made very clear that no gentleman would allow much of his time or thought to be concerned with money making, and a good city should teach its citizens to have contempt for mere economics—since economics is concerned with survival, a necessary but low concern. Machiavelli suggested the opposite. Since human beings are restless and acquisitive, a more stable society can be constructed by *letting* men devote themselves to what they really care about—making money. Instead of constantly fighting this tendency to materialism, as Aristotle's moral education would seek to do, Machiavelli urged giving in to it.

The ancient political science taught that the aim of a political community is the "common good" of all the citizens, the name for which is justice. But Machiavelli suggested that there is no such thing as a "common good"—all there ever can be are individual, private goods, since man is individual by nature. Men live in societies not, as the ancients thought, because only in societies can men be fully human, but because societies offer them security and protection for their lives and goods, which are the only needs they have, inside or outside a community. Justice, Machiavelli implied, is only a name for how goods are distributed, and the best policy is to increase the supply of actual material goods rather than seek some illusory, nonmaterial "common good." Political communities should be understood as collections of individuals, each seeking his own private good. This is a direct and explicit contradiction of Aristotle's famous statement that a *polis* "is not merely an association of residents on a common site, for purposes of trade and commerce."[3] Aristotle rejected that idea as too low because it reduces man to his animal needs. But Machiavelli taught us to admit that man *is* only an animal, not some sort of "political being" whose nature is between those of the beasts and the gods. Aristotle said that although a *polis* may "come into being for the sake of mere life, it exists—once in existence—for the sake of the *good* life,"[4] which is higher. Machiavelli denied the reality of any such notion: survival and security are the aims of political communities, as of the individuals who people them.

Machiavelli is also the first *democratic* political philosopher. And his reasons are consistent with what we've just seen. In *The Prince*—ostensibly a book of advice for princes—he teaches the potential prince to base his power on the common people, because "they are easier to satisfy."[5] Because the common people care only about being left alone (to pursue wealth and protect their families and property), a prince who bases his power on them will find

[3] Aristotle, *Politics*, Book 3, Ch. 4.

[4] *Ibid.,* Book I, Ch. 2.

[5] Niccolo Machiavelli, *The Prince*, translated by Mark Musa (New York: St. Martin's Press, 1964), Ch. 9.

his rule more stable and secure. The "low" aims of life (as Plato would have called them) are more easily taken care of, and the statesman who sees this—and encourages subjects to aim low—will have a long and secure reign. Aristotle favored aristocracy precisely because the tone of political life is higher in an aristocracy. He favored excluding from political life those whose lives had been concerned with making money, with trade and commerce. The high goals of the leisured few—virtue, glory, nobility—give rise to a political life of emulation and competition, which are the ingredients for instability and turmoil.

We can summarize Machiavelli's revolutionary understanding of politics by saying that he offered a radically new political science. It's not that the ancients didn't see the tendency of men to be preoccupied by animal needs and low goals; but those tendencies, they thought, must be combated if man is to flower in all his human potential. Machiavelli rejected this as idealistic, and offered a lower, more "realistic" view of human nature and politics as the basis for a new conception of society. The goal of political life is not virtue, or salvation, or glory, but security and prosperity. A ruler should "encourage his subjects to enable them to pursue their trades in tranquillity, whether they be in commerce, agriculture, or any other trade a man may have; so that one man will not be afraid to enrich his possessions for fear that they will be taken from him, while another will not be afraid to engage in commerce through fear of taxes."[6]

One more thing: Machiavelli's realism is not pessimistic. In fact there is a kind of optimism in Machiavelli that is surprising in one who seems so cynical. The classical political philosophers taught men to think about what is highest and best, but they also taught moderation. Precisely because what is highest is rare and difficult, a wise statesman should not expect to achieve the "best city." Human affairs depend too much on fortune for us to expect the full flowering of human potential. In a famous chapter at the end of *The Prince*, Machiavelli speculated on "how much fortune can do in human affairs"[7] and offered a theoretical reflection on human power and freedom. He suggested, with breathtaking audacity, that if men will shed their fatalism about fortune, their resignation about what can be achieved, and begin to regard nature as an enemy to be conquered, then the limiting conditions that forced Aristotle to recommend moderation can be overcome. For example, if we cease to see philosophy as an example of what is highest and best in man, enjoyable for its own sake, and start to view it as only a tool to be used to improve life, we can actually change the world. The classics had resisted making use of the mind—

[6] *Ibid,* Ch. 21, p. 191.
[7] *Ibid,* Ch. 25, p. 209.

man's highest faculty—merely as a means to low ends. Machiavelli urged us to take reason off its pedestal and make it a tool for the conquest of nature and the satisfaction of our bodily needs. He thus pointed the way to the development of modern natural science, whose aim, in the words of its great founder Francis Bacon, is to serve for "the relief of man's estate."[8]

We have focused on Machiavelli in this chapter because so much of the modern liberal understanding of man, morals, and politics can be traced to his revolutionary ideas. The following chapters show how parts of his teaching were transformed into new shapes that formed the building blocks of liberal commercial society. Once the new view took firm root in the West—a process that took several centuries—the lofty classical understanding of man became hard to grasp. For the societies of the West, at least, the purpose of political life was radically altered, and with it a new world became possible.

[8]Francis Bacon, "The Proficience and Advancement of Learning Divine and Humane" in *Francis Bacon: A Selection,* edited by Sidney Warhaft (Indianapolis: Bobbs-Merrill, 1981), p. 235.

Chapter 6

SCIENCE, AMBITION,
AND CONQUEST

The preceeding chapter dealt with the radically new understanding of man and politics introduced in the early sixteenth century by Niccolo Machiavelli, who challenged the classical view of human nature and the basis for political community which had been accepted in one form or another for nearly two thousand years. But one particular side of Machiavelli's understanding—the side connected to the political ambition of princely men—was barely touched. Some human beings care more about glory and dominion over others than about prosperity or bodily security. According to Machiavelli, these are the only human beings who are devoted primarily to political activity, and there aren't very many of them. As Machiavelli sees it, the ancients mistakenly claimed that man is a political being by nature because the ancients thought the few (whom we might call the princely men)

should be taken as the standard for all men, even though most people care only about prosperity (and about family or domestic life) and not about honor, glory, dominion, or fame.

Machiavelli seems to be saying that a happy combination of these two basic types of human beings is possible: the honor-seeking ruler can win fame and glory by ruling well, so long as he knows that most people care more about prosperity than about honor. In Machiavelli's pithy formulation, the wise prince must "above all… abstain from what belongs to others, for men forget more quickly the death of their fathers than the loss of their patrimony."[1] But the threat to liberty and peace posed by politically ambitious men may be a more difficult problem to solve than Machiavelli perceived. Thus some of his successors thought deeply about this and proposed other solutions.

The most important suggestion may well have been advanced by Francis Bacon, the great English statesman and philosopher who lived a century after Machiavelli and who was one of his greatest students. Bacon is generally regarded as the founder of modern natural science, and his proposal concerning ambition is part of his great project for a new kind of philosophy. Bacon proposed redirecting the forces of human ambition, which throughout human

---

[1] Machiavelli, *The Prince,* Ch 17, p. 139.

history had generally been channeled into political conquest and building empires. In Bacon's view, we should distinguish among "three kinds and, as it were, grades of ambition in mankind." The lowest or first is that of "those who desire to extend their own power in their native country." This kind of ambition Bacon dismisses as "vulgar and degenerate." More admirable is the second: the ambition "of those who labour to extend the power of their country and its dominion among men." In this class we would presumably place the ambition of men such as Alexander the Great or Julius Caesar. Their ambition, compared to the first sort, "certainly has more dignity, though not less covetousness." Bacon continues: "But if a man endeavor to establish and extend the power and dominion of the human race itself over the universe, his ambition (if ambition it can be called) is without doubt both a more wholesome thing and a more noble than the other two. Now the empire of man over things depends wholly on the arts and sciences."[2]

Part of what has been called Bacon's "project of progress"[3] is thus to persuade men and women of great ambition to devote their talents and capacities to the conquest not of nations, but of nature. Like Machiavelli,

---

[2] *The New Organon* CXXIX, in Warhaft. *Francis Bacon: A Selection of His Works*, p. 374

[3] Robert K. Faulkner, *Francis Bacon and the Project of Progress* (Lanham, Md.: Rowman and Littlefield Publishers, 1993).

Bacon saw himself as seeking "to open a new way for the understanding."[4] Bacon was explicit about his goal of establishing a new kind of philosophy or science devoted to the mastery of nature and the improvement of human life, and he was confident of its potential benefits as compared with improvements in law or government. "For the benefits of discoveries may extend to the whole race of man, civil benefits only to particular places; the latter last not beyond a few ages, the former through all time. Moreover, the reformation of a state in civil matters is seldom brought in without violence and confusion; but discoveries carry blessings with them, and confer benefits without causing harm or sorrow to any."[5]

What stands in the way of such discoveries, or of the progress Bacon thinks possible? On this too Bacon is very clear. "Men have been kept back as by a kind of enchantment from progress in the sciences by reverence for antiquity, by the authority of men accounted great in philosophy."[6] Bacon saw as his first task to cultivate dissatisfaction, that is, to bring others to share his low estimate of the state of learning and philosophy, and so to launch an attack on the classical virtue of moderation. Moderation meant (to philosophers) that they should seek

[4] Warhaft, *Francis Bacon: A Selection of His Works,* p. 328.

[5] *Ibid.,* p. 373.

[6] *Ibid.,* p. 356.

to know the highest things, or the best state of things, but should not expect to see the best or highest realized in this imperfect world. Both Christian thought and the philosophy (or quasi-religion) of the Stoics counseled resignation or moderation in respect to the ills that plague human life: disease, famine, injustice. Ancient or classical reflection taught men and women to accept these worldly ills as inevitable, part of the nature of things, since the natural world is ordained by God or the gods.

But Francis Bacon was not moderate, and he was not satisfied. The opinion that things are all right, according to Bacon, "is one of the chief causes of want." His most systematic work outlining the project of a new science thus begins with a ringing declaration: it is "not only useful, but absolutely necessary, that the excess of honour and admiration with which our existing stock of inventions is regarded, be in the very entrance and threshold of the work, and that frankly and without circumlocution, stripped off, and men be duly warned not to exaggerate or make too much of them."[7] Anyone who looks carefully at the books that contain the arts and sciences handed down to us, he says, will find only endless disputes and arguments, without "value and utility."

Bacon hopes to eliminate complacency about the state of learning, and to replace it with a new spirit of adven-

[7] *Ibid,* p. 302.

ture and challenge. "By far the greatest obstacle to the progress of science and to the undertaking of new tasks...is found in this—that men despair and think things impossible."[8] His writings are meant to spur others on and to "whet their industry," and he compares himself to Columbus, whose bold voyage persuaded others that there were worlds to be discovered. He proposed, in short, a spirit of *progress*.

But what does Bacon's project have to do with liberty? Why is his vision of a new science—and the progress it would bring—important in this study of the foundational ideas of free societies? To see the answer, we need only take seriously Bacon's own claims, and that is easy to do when we look back over the centuries. In Bacon's time the physical circumstances of human life (the tools, the food, the sanitary conditions, the sicknesses, even the likelihood of famine or plague) were not all that much different from what they had been for two thousand years. Except for the very rich, most of the life of every man, woman, and child was spent in drudgery, in what might be called "bondage to necessity." Even for the very rich, human habitations were *uncomfortable*: houses (and castles) were cold and dark, smoky and smelly in winter. A chamber pot may be preferable to an outdoor privy, but is still a far cry from a flush toilet in a warm, clean bathroom.

[8] *Ibid.*, p. 358.

The "miseries and necessities" of human life are surely obstacles to human freedom in the most basic sense of liberation from drudgery and toil. And modern natural science, as the visionary Bacon taught, would contribute greatly to "the relief of man's estate" and thus to the increase of an important kind of freedom, freedom from want, from anxiety, and from bondage to our most basic bodily needs. Freedom from material necessity may be one of the least exalted kinds of freedom, but it is nonetheless important.

Of course science alone did not bring material progress, which depends partly on political and economic circumstances (as we have already seen). But without something like Bacon's project, his redirection of human ambition, and his kindling of an adventurous spirit aimed at the conquest of nature, it seems unlikely that the fantastic progress in the improvement of the material circumstances of human life could have taken place. Bacon was far from the only great thinker involved in promulgating what has been called "the modern project." René Descartes, Galileo Galilei, William Harvey, and many other "founders of modern natural science" fall into this category.

Some other aspects of the connection between science and freedom deserve to be mentioned. One of the most important is surely the Baconian connection between human ambition and material progress. It is a common misconception today that rich nations are rich somehow because other nations are poor, as if at one time all were in a sort of middling condition and now wealth has flowed from the areas we call poor to those we call rich. But a moment's reflection on history shows why this is mistaken: as Bacon knew, without human efforts and human progress, the human condition—materially speaking—is one of misery, marked by poverty, disease, and want. In some places or nations there has been *progress,* while in others the primitive conditions have yet to be transcended. Wealth and freedom from material necessity result from human creative efforts, which depend in part on a sense of what human beings can indeed accomplish and in part on establishing the institutions favorable to liberty and progress. Bacon's great contribution was to persuade his countrymen that they need not "settle for" the material conditions which had always seemed to be simply part of being human.

The American founders, a century and a half after Bacon's death, took very seriously the notion of progress and the importance of science, which we have traced to the great English statesman. The American founders were not romantic about the natural condition of human life, and did not wish to return to a simple and pure state of harmony with nature. They were proponents of science (Benjamin Franklin is one famous example) and had great faith in the benefits of progress and invention—so much so that they enshrined in the U. S. Constitution a provision to encourage inventors, in the form of the U. S. Patent Office. The faith in science as a guarantor of progress and an important contributor to human freedom continued to be robust in America for two centuries, but in the last part of the twentieth century, voices expressing doubt have been raised. This leads to other important reflections on science and freedom.

One view of modern natural science seems, at least, to tell against human freedom by undermining the very possibility of free human agency. According to this view (that is, to the critics of science who view it this way), scientific explanation is causal explanation and is consistent only with a deterministic view of the universe. A deterministic view holds that all events are caused: they are somehow entailed by their causes and could not happen in any other way than they do happen. So if we explain human behavior scientifically or causally, we deprive human beings of something they have always believed in, namely, their possession of free will. Those who take this view claim that freedom is (and always was) only an illusion, which natural science has now dispelled. One famous psychologist wrote a book entitled *Beyond Freedom and Dignity,* which argued that freedom and dignity are old-fashioned notions that can now be dispensed with, since behavioral psychology will soon be able to explain the causes that determine all human behavior. Adherents of this view are in a minority, however, and the persuasiveness of their claim seems to be waning as human powers—genetic manipulation, for example—raise ever more serious moral questions about what looks rather like radically free human will.

This points to another serious issue, the relation between science and religion. Whatever the proper relation between these two, it cannot be denied that in Bacon's time they were understood by many on both sides to be antagonists or competitors as "teachings about the universe." And of course Bacon was aware of the tension. The Copernican system was rejected by Church authorities as an explanation of the solar system, and in 1615–16 the great Italian astronomer and physicist Galileo Galilei was under investigation by the Holy Office for heretical writings (the famous trial, in which he was forced to recant his teachings, took place in 1633). The attitude of at least some scientist-philosophers to the teachings of the Church on matters of physics or astronomy was nicely captured by Thomas Hobbes, who offered the following succinct if provocative definition: "Feare of power invisible, feigned by the mind, or imagined from tales publicly allowed, RELIGION; not allowed, SUPERSTITION."[9] The antagonism between Christianity and natural science, seen so clearly in this early period, may be unfortunate, but history is history.

[9] Thomas Hobbes, *Leviathan*, Ch. 6.

Bacon was sensitive to the tension, and tried to forestall criticism by insisting that his project was not in any way meant to step on theological toes. Citing as his authority King Solomon, author of *Proverbs*, he wrote that "of the sciences which regard nature, the divine philosopher declares that 'it is the glory of God to conceal a thing, but it is the glory of the King to find a thing out.'"[10] In his great fable *The New Atlantis*, in which Bacon sketched a society which has enjoyed the benefits of something like Baconian natural science for nearly two thousand years, he is careful to insist that the entire society is highly religious. Indeed, its central and most striking features seem to be the Christian virtues of humanity, mercy, and chastity, and it is marked by what we might call a Puritanical morality. Yet Bacon describes the scientific foundation (Salomon's House, or the College of Six Days' Works) as a secretive and hidden organization: the society of Bensalem (as the New Atlantis is known) enjoys all the fruits of science without any public evidence of the scientists' research work. Whether this is because Bacon thought the moral structure necessary to a rich and free society would be undermined by openly practiced natural science is diffi-cult to tell. Surely it indicates that he thought science might be dangerous if not controlled or regulated by moral or political considerations, even if these are con-

[10] Warhaft, *Francis Bacon: A Selection of His Works,* p. 310.

cerns only or primarily of scientists themselves. It may well be that a free society is especially in need of the moral guidelines of a religion such as Christianity, which teaches the sanctity of human life and the duty to love one's neighbor. And indeed, many great scientists, including Isaac Newton, perhaps the greatest physicist who ever lived, were profoundly religious.

One final observation—of great importance today—about the relation of science to freedom: the belief that freedom and truth are closely related was once a commonplace in Western civilization, not least because of Jesus' famous pronouncement that "you shall know the truth and the truth shall make you free."[11] When truth is manipulated by political leaders, or when people believe that there is no truth (as is maintained by "nihilists"), it seems obvious that human beings are slaves to illusions or shadows. At the very least, if there is no truth it is impossible to "speak truth to power."

A century after Friedrich Nietzsche announced that God is dead and declared that "nihilism stands at the door," universities are only too familiar with the influential intellectual movement known as postmodernism, a form of radical relativism that holds that truth is always the creation of those in power, of the dominant class or race or nation, which, by virtue of its position of power,

[11] John 8:32.

gets to declare what "truth" is. According to this view life is always a struggle for power and power is the only reality; truth is just whatever the winners in the struggle for power say it is. In any society there is a power structure, and those on the bottom are fooled into accepting it because the powerful say "this is the way it is." But of course in this view no one can speak truth to power: there is no truth outside of the struggle for power. And that means there is no freedom—or there is freedom only for the powerful.

The modern science of nature, which is an outgrowth of the centuries-old quest for truth about the nature of things, has of course always understood itself as an enterprise seeking truth, about nature as a whole as well as human nature (postmodernists claim that there is no human nature, and that what was once called human nature is only a "social construction," specific to a particular time and place). Thus modern natural science is connected to truth as intimately as can be, and connected to freedom insofar as freedom and truth are related. In universities today, the "hard sciences" still maintain a strong commitment to truth and to objective standards, while it is the humanities departments that harbor the radical nihilists, the postmodernists who deny that there is such a thing as truth. Thus the scientist who believes he or she is pursuing truth is regarded by the postmodern deconstructionist as not quite up to date, as still in the grip of an old-fashioned conviction that truth can be found. The final chapter deals further with this issue of the connection between truth and freedom.

Chapter 7

NATURAL RIGHTS AND
THE NATURAL CONDITION

In the previous chapter we saw how the project of modern natural science, associated with the great English statesman Francis Bacon, grew out of the radically new understanding of man and of nature that had been launched a century earlier by Niccolo Machiavelli. Now we turn to the thought of another of the great successors to Machiavelli, Thomas Hobbes (at one time a secretary to Francis Bacon). More than any other single philosopher, Hobbes is responsible for using the new principles of Machiavelli as a foundation on which to erect the scaffolding of modern liberal political philosophy. The crucial features of Machiavelli's teaching—that man is by nature individual, not political; that nature is not a benevolent mother but a hostile force which man must overcome; that reason and philosophy are not the highest, god-like part of man, but rather merely tools to be used to ensure survival and improve life—all were accepted by Hobbes even as he transformed them and used them to develop the theoretical underpinnings of modern free societies consisting of individuals living in peace and seeking to satisfy their own desires.

Hobbes was born at Malmesbury, in England, in 1588, and was educated at Oxford in the early 1600s. To understand his thought it helps to recall what was happening in the northwestern European states in the first half of the seventeenth century. One of the by-products of the Protestant Reformation a century before Hobbes, as we saw, was the sectarian strife that ripped European society apart in the early decades of the seventeenth century. The Thirty Years War pitted Catholic rulers against Protestant princes in a war that raged across much of Europe. In England, the Stuarts had come to the throne in 1603 when James VI of Scotland became King James I of England. James was officially allied with the English or Anglican Church, but more radical Protestants, the Puritans, dominated Parliament. Certainly religious disagreements were not the only causes of the century of turmoil England suffered during Hobbes's life, but they were never absent as England was plunged into civil war. James's own son, Charles I, was put to death in 1649, and England was declared a republic, known as the Commonwealth, led by the Puritan Oliver Cromwell. The damage to English civil order was very grave, however,

and the Stuarts were restored to the English throne in
1660, with the nation reverting to the Anglican religion.

The English civil war is the setting against which to
view Hobbes's two great preoccupations: peace as the goal
of civil order, and a new political science as the means to
that goal. Hobbes is quite clear about his central concern:
"Now all such calamities as may be avoided by human
industry, arise from war, but chiefly from civil war; for
from this proceed slaughter, solitude, and the want of all
things. But the cause of war is not that men are willing to
have it; for the will has nothing for object but good, at
least that which seemeth good."[1] What, then, leads men
into civil war? "The cause, therefore, of civil war," Hobbes
continues, "is, that men know not the causes neither of
war nor peace, there being but few in the world that have
learned those duties which unite and keep men in
peace."[2] And the study of causes is precisely the task of
philosophy. The most important philosophy, according to
Hobbes, is that by which men learn "the rules of civil life."
"Now, the knowledge of these rules is moral philosophy,"
Hobbes says. "But why have they not learned them, unless
for this reason, that none hitherto have taught them in a
clear and exact method?"[3]

---

[1] Thomas Hobbes, *De Corpore*, I. 1.7.

[2] *Ibid.*

[3] *Ibid.*

Thus Hobbes's lifelong ambition was to establish the first genuine political science, which by "a clear and exact method" would establish the basis for any legitimate civil order. He studied very carefully the emerging natural science of Galileo and Descartes, great continental philosopher-scientists, and applied the method of science to the study of man. He believed that if he could achieve a truly scientific understanding of human nature, it would be possible to show how natural needs lead men to constitute political society in order to satisfy their prepolitical, natural needs—namely self-preservation, security, and the means for "commodious living." It is important to grasp that Hobbes intended his science to apply to *all* human beings, to men and women in any cultural or historical setting. To do this he believed that science must strip away all merely cultural or historical accretions and study human beings as they exist *before* particular customs or societies distort or influence human behavior.

Hobbes believed political science could *not* begin from the answers different cultures have given to the question, "How should men live?" for the disagreements about the answers are precisely what give rise to war and even civil war. All Hobbes's predecessors, he wrote, failed to use the scientific method because they grounded their political philosophies on authoritative claims different cultures make about justice, virtue, or salvation—things about which men will always disagree. "They that have written about justice and policy in general, do all invade each other, and themselves, with contradiction," Hobbes wrote. "To reduce this doctrine to the rules and infallibility of reason," he said of political science, "there is no way, but first to put such principles down for a foundation, as passion not mistrusting, may not seek to displace."[4]

So Hobbes went searching for the simple principles all could agree on, to use as the foundation for his political science. All genuine sciences, he observed, proceed by finding the simplest elements out of which more complex things are composed. Once these elements are defined or understood clearly, we can combine them, by constructing theoretical models, to explain the more complicated wholes. Thus the botanist understands a tree as a combination of cells of different kinds, which combine to explain the properties of wood, leaves, and so on. And the cells in turn are all composed of a few simpler elements— mostly carbon, hydrogen, and oxygen—combined in various ways. Classical political science, Hobbes believed, was as misguided as classical physics, because both sought to understand things in light of their ends or completions or goals, rather than by breaking them down into their constituent parts.

[4] Thomas Hobbes, *The Elements of Law*, "The Epistle Dedicatory" (London: Cass & Co., 1969), p. xv.

Since political science tries to understand the proper order for political community, Hobbes suggested seeing the community as a collection of more basic elements: human individuals. If we want to know the proper structure of the large whole, we must look at how a community comes into being out of its elements or constituent parts. But first we must understand the parts. What makes human beings tick? If we can't agree on this, our political science will get us nowhere. We can't begin to explain human behavior as Aristotle did by looking at ends, or goals, or virtues. "For one man calleth wisdom," Hobbes says, "what another calleth fear, and one cruelty, what another justice,"[5] and so on. "And therefore such names can never be true grounds"[6] of any science. Men do not agree about ends or goals, Hobbes goes on, so we must begin somewhere else. So he based his political science on a reductive psychology which attempted to explain all human behavior in terms of a few "simples." All human behavior, he argued, can be understood as motion. And there are only two kinds of voluntary motion: motion toward and motion away from. These he called "appetite" and "aversion." By focusing on motion itself and not its goal, we can find a point of agreement! Who can disagree with the proposition that life is motion? "And because the

[5] Hobbes, *Leviathan*, Ch.4, p. 22.
[6] *Ibid*.

constitution of a man's body," Hobbes asserted, "is in continual mutation; it is impossible that all the same things
should always cause in him the same appetites and aversions: much less can all men consent, in the desire of
almost any one and the same object. But whatsoever is the
object of any man's appetite or desire; that is it, which he
for his part calleth *good*: And the object of his hate, and
aversion, *evil*; and of his contempt, *vile* and *inconsiderable*.
For these words of good, evil, and contemptible, are ever
used with relation to the person that useth them: There
being nothing simply and absolutely so."[7]

Starting from this basis of agreement, Hobbes proceeds
to build a comprehensive psychology to explain human
behavior. Each man—whatever his religion or his goals—
is a bundle of "appetites and aversions." Each seeks his
own good. The power of this reductionist explanation is
that it compels agreement, since whatever else one can say
about man, this approach can explain *anything*. Who can
disagree? Even the altruist's selfless behavior is after all but
an attempt to move in a way he defines as good! Once we
can explain human behavior as resulting from a bundle of
appetites and aversions, we can bring the elements of society together and see what happens. We presume nothing
at all here about laws or customs or religions or anything
else, since we want to know what is the *minimum* condi-

---

[7] *Ibid.*, pp. 28-29.

tion, the basic situation, for any human being. What political science is seeking, in other words, is a picture of what
Hobbes called the "State of Nature"—the condition
human beings would be in if and if all the conventions and
laws of political society were dissolved (or the condition
human beings were in before laws were invented).

Now, the mutability of human desires has already been
noted, and Hobbes considers this a key feature of his
political science because no one can accuse him of pre-
suming any conception of "the good life." Precisely
because every man's desires are ever-changing, however, a
man finds it hard to plan for tomorrow. Yet, Hobbes points
out, there is something a man can seek today that will help
him tomorrow *whatever* his desires may be: he can seek
power, which Hobbes defines as "the present means to
obtain some future apparent good."[8] (The most common
forms of power in society are wealth and reputation.) But
since power is by definition scarce, Hobbes predicts that
competition will result when men seek it. According to
him this is simply a logically necessary part of the state of
nature: "So that in the first place, I put for a general inclination of all mankind, a perpetual and restless desire of
power after power, that ceaseth only in death."[9] And who
can disagree, after all, since "the cause of this, is not always
that a man hopes for a more intensive delight, than he has

[8] *Ibid.,* p. 50.
[9] *Ibid.,* p. 58.

already attained to; or that he cannot be content with a moderate power: but because he cannot assure the power and means to live well, which he hath present, without the acquisition of more."[10]

One more feature of the state of nature is of crucial importance in order to understand Hobbes's full account of the purpose of political life. This crucial feature is the fundamental *equality* of human beings, in the political sense. Hobbes made no attempt to claim men are equal in talent, or ability, or intelligence, but, he argued, men are equal politically:

> Nature has made men so equal, in the faculties of body, and mind; as that though there be found one man some-times manifestly stronger in body, or of quicker mind than another; yet when all is reckoned together, the difference between man, and man, is not so considerable, as that one man can thereupon claim to himself any benefit, to which another may not pretend, as well as he. For as to strength of body, the weakest has strength enough to kill the strongest, either by secret machination, or by confederacy with others, that are in the same danger with himself.[11]

That is, no one can be viewed as politically superior, because every human being is vulnerable to violent death at the hands of his fellows, even if they must act in concert. In the state of nature, anyone who tries to enslave or rule

[10] *Ibid.*

[11] *Ibid.,* p. 74.

another will not survive long, because even a strong man must sleep. Thus, our fundamental equality in vulnerability forces us to admit political equality.

But from equality, Hobbes says, "proceeds diffidence, and from diffidence, war."[12] The state of nature must have been a terrible condition, a "war of everyman against everyman,"[13] at least in principle. War, Hobbes says, consists not only in actual fighting, but in the disposition to fight, and where there is no ruler and no law, men must fight or perish. Hobbes's description of the natural condition of mankind is justly famous, and should be thought about carefully, for he intends us to learn that this is what men face, always and everywhere, when they dissolve or destroy the rule of law and fall into the savage conditions of the prepolitical state of nature: "In such condition, there is no place for industry; because the fruit thereof is uncertain; and consequently no culture of the earth; no navigation, nor use of the commodities that may be imported by sea; no commodious building; no instruments of moving, and removing such things as require much force; no knowledge of the face of the earth; no account of time; no arts; no letters; no society; and which is worst of all, continual fear, and danger of violent death; and the life of man, solitary, poor, nasty, brutish, and short."[14]

This fearful state of nature is the fundamental condition

[12] *Ibid,* p. 75.

[13] *Ibid,* p. 76.

[14] *Ibid.,* p. 76.

of mankind, according to Hobbes, even though appearances might suggest otherwise. Precisely because the natural condition is so dreadful, Hobbes suggests, we rarely see it: men are quickly driven into society as a way of escaping the desperate, hand-to-mouth existence they confront outside of a social order. But if human beings are no more than bundles of passions, of what Hobbes calls "appetites and aversions," how can men ever find a way out of so fearful a condition? The key, Hobbes teaches, is exactly its fearfulness: when men and women are moved by so powerful a passion as fear, their reason—even if only a servant of the passions—will show them a way to escape from the fear, by discovering for them what Hobbes calls "natural laws." "A LAW OF NATURE *(lex naturalis),*" he writes, "is a precept, or general rule, found out by reason, by which a man is forbidden to do that which is destructive of his life, or taketh away the means of preserving the same; and to omit, that, by which he thinketh it may be best preserved." The first law of nature is to "seek peace."[15]

In the natural condition, self-preservation is every person's major concern, and where there are no laws laid down, everyone has a natural right to anything—and everything—which will help him preserve his life. There are no limits. But such unlimited rights are necessarily *very* insecure, since everyone has a right in principle to every-

[15] *Ibid.,* pp. 79-80.

thing. Note that according to Hobbes and later liberal thinkers, the true ground of all individual rights is the natural need to preserve oneself. The laws of nature teach man to "*be willing, when others are so too, as far-forth as for peace, and defence of himself he shall think it necessary, to lay down this right to all things, and be contented with so much liberty against other men, as he would allow other men against himself.*"[16]

Hobbes sums this up by saying that the laws of nature teach us to give up some of our rights, as long as other men do so as well, and to create a fictional *person*, called the sovereign, to assume the rights we renounce, chief among which is the right to punish those whom we think are a threat to us. Hobbes calls this agreement a "covenant" because it is an open-ended contract, a promise that must be continually fulfilled in the future. But alas, he notes, "covenants without the sword are but words,"[17] or empty promises, unless someone is there to enforce them. This problem suggests a second major duty for the sovereign: to ensure, by threat of force, the continued performance of the covenant itself. Hobbes is careful to emphasize that the sovereign is a fictional person, not a real one. It is created by the act of covenanting, to "represent" or "act for" all the individuals who are parties to the

[16] *Ibid.*, p. 80.
[17] *Ibid.*, p. 106.

contract and who thus can be said to "authorize" all that the sovereign does. The sovereign is not a real person, but may be "borne by" a real man, or by an assembly of men, either large or small. If the sovereignty rests in a large assembly constituting a majority, we say that the commonwealth is a democracy—a form of government Hobbes thought unworkable and dangerous. But the only legitimate basis for any civil order, according to Hobbes, is a covenant that creates a sovereign. If men cannot be understood to have voluntarily consented to the creation of a sovereign, and the civil society it governs, then they remain in a state of war with all others.

The thought of John Locke, taken up in due course, will explain this in more detail. Here we can summarize some of the basic features of the liberal understanding of civil society:

(1) Individuals are understood to be prior to, and more fundamental than, any social order.

(2) The natural need for self-preservation is the only true reason men live in political communities. That is, political communities exist to satisfy *individual*, prepolitical needs of human nature, including life, security, and the means to what Hobbes calls "commodious living."

(3) Because these needs are universal and scientifically demonstrable for all men and women, they offer a basis for agreement and a peaceful political order.

(4) Since political society exists for self-preservation, no man can ever give up the right to defend himself. For example, it is a cardinal principle of liberal society that no man can be compelled to confess a crime or to testify against or incriminate himself in court.

(5) All legitimate government rests on a contract consented to, at least tacitly, by individuals; no one can consent for anyone but himself. The sovereign is a legal "person" who represents all the individuals, acting for them in whatever he does.

The last principle, as we will see, justified a very powerful government or sovereign, which Hobbes thought necessary to prevent civil war, the greatest calamity that can befall men. But this principle was soon challenged by Hobbes's great successor, John Locke, who argued that even the sovereign must be limited.

Chapter 8

PROPERTY AND LIBERTY

Here we consider the philosophical teaching of John Locke, whose name is or should be identified with the principles of modern liberal society wherever it is talked about. It was Locke more than any other individual who expressed the basic understanding of man, nature, and society that underlies the type of society that consists of free individuals freely pursuing their chosen ends. Many of the building blocks of Locke's vision have been noted in the thought of Machiavelli and Hobbes, but it was Locke who managed, by means of an astounding feat of rhetoric, to put them in such a form that respectable men and women could think and talk about them openly. This allowed the principles of modern liberal individualism to become political watchwords, to appear in political manifestos, and to be heard in public speeches.

Why was such a rhetorical accomplishment necessary?

Locke's predecessors had taught that a more peaceful and secure political order could be constructed if political theorists and statesmen could be brought to lower their expectations, to admit that civil society does not exist for man's perfection or for the sake of virtue, but merely to satisfy low, animal needs: survival and security. In this view man is only an animal, and nature is an enemy to be conquered. Man is not, in short, political by nature as the classical and Christian traditions had taught. These new views were regarded as scandalous by the Church authorities and by rulers who grounded their power on what James I defended as the "divine right of kings." Machiavelli's name had already become synonymous with cynicism and deception. Thomas Hobbes was widely regarded as an atheist, and his championing of the method of the new natural science did not contribute to his respectability, since the Church was at odds with the new science in many respects. Hobbes's teaching about the fearful and desperate natural condition of mankind was the clearest example of what was not respectable in his philosophy.

How did Locke manage to overcome the public antipathy and make such principles not only respectable but popular? This was his rhetorical achievement. He began his most important political work, the *Second Treatise of Civil Government*, by distancing himself from those who teach that "all government in the World is the product only of Force and Violence, and that Men live together by no other rules but that of Beasts,"[1] and appears to offer a quite different account of the state of nature, suggesting it is actually full of peace and friendship.

To begin with, he denies—on the surface—Hobbes's equation of the state of nature with a state of war. Locke writes, "And here we have the plain *difference between the state of Nature, and the State of War,* which however some Men have confounded, are as far distant, as a State of Peace, Good Will, Mutual Assistance, and Preservation, and a State of Enmity, Malice, Violence, and Mutual Destruction are one from another. Men living together according to reason, without a common Superior on Earth, with Authority to judge between them, is *properly the State of Nature.*"[2] But even as he presents this much more congenial teaching on the surface of his writing, he surreptitiously supplies the grounds to show that Hobbes was right. The casual reader sees only the surface teaching, but Locke contrives his text so that a careful reader will be troubled by minor contradictions, or hints about "this strange doctrine," and be led to penetrate beneath the soothing claims about the natural condition. And many pages later Locke admits what he had earlier covered over, namely, that the state of nature is an intolerable condition, "full of fears and continual dangers." That is precisely why

[1] John Locke, *Two Treatises of Government*, edited by Peter Laslett (Cambridge: Cambridge University Press, 1960), *Second Treatise,* Par. 1, p. 308.

[2] *Ibid.,* Par. 19, p. 321.

men flee it and form societies. "If Man in the State of Nature be so free," he says, "as has been said; If he be absolute Lord of his own Person and Possessions, equal to the greatest, and subject to no Body, why will he part with his Freedom? Why will he give up this Empire, and sub-ject himself to the Dominion and Control of any other Power? To which 'tis obvious to Answer, that though in the state of Nature he hath such a right, yet the Enjoyment of it is very uncertain, and constantly exposed to the Invasion of others."[3]

By hiding the uglier parts of Hobbes's understanding of man's natural condition, Locke managed to make the understanding itself acceptable and even respectable. Man could be understood as radically individual, owing no duties to community or others, and oriented chiefly by the natural need for self-preservation in a hostile environ-ment. This allowed Locke to explain that men form soci-eties—and acquire duties by renouncing some of their limitless but insecure rights—"for the mutual *Preservation* of their Lives, Liberties, and Estates, which I call by the general Name, *Property*."[4]

And here Locke goes beyond his great predecessors. His account of property, its grounding in nature, and its unavoidably private character, is the most important part

[3] *Ibid.,* Par. 123, p. 395.
[4] *Ibid.*

of his contribution to the ideas underlying liberal commercial society. But here too there was an obstacle to overcome, in the long tradition of misunderstandings of wealth and human economic activity, often associated with the Church and the medieval scholastic outlook. So Locke resorted to another brilliant rhetorical strategy in his famous chapter on property. He presented, on the surface, an account that seemed to accord with the traditional view, while underneath the surface he managed to show a quite different picture.

Both views depend, first, on the same account of the origin of property. By nature, Locke wrote, material things are not owned by anyone but exist in common for all men. "God, as King *David* says, (Psalm 115:16) *has given the Earth to the Children of Men,* given it to Mankind in common."[5] Yet each individual has a natural need to preserve himself, and to preserve his life every human being must eat. All men, Locke said, by nature "have a Right to their Preservation and consequently to Meat, and Drink, and such other things, as Nature affords for their Subsistence."[6] Thus even though all things are given by God to men in common, "yet being given for the use of Men there must of necessity be a means to appropriate them some way or other before they can be of any use, or

[5] *Ibid.,* Par. 25, p. 327.
[6] *Ibid.*

at all beneficial to any particular Man. The Fruit, or Venison, which nourishes the wild Indian, who knows no Inclosure, and is still a Tenant in common, must be his, and so his, i.e. part of him, that another can no longer have any right to it, before it can do him any good for the support of his Life."[7] And Locke is perfectly plain as to how this occurs. "Though the Earth, and all inferior Creatures be common to all Men, yet every Man has a *Property* in his own *Person*. This no Body has any Right to but himself. The *Labour* of his Body, and the *Work* of his Hands, we may say, are properly his. Whatsoever then he removes out of the state that nature hath provided, and left it in, he hath mixed his *Labour* with, and joyned to it something that is his own, and thereby makes it his *Property.*"[8]

And Locke rebuts potential objections with a simple line of reasoning: "He that is nourished by the Acorns he pickt up under an Oak, or the Apples he gathered from the Trees in the Wood, has certainly appropriated them to himself. No Body can deny but the nourishment is his. I ask then, When did they begin to be his? When he digested? Or when he eat? Or when he boiled? Or when he brought them home? Or when he pickt them up? And 'tis plain, if the first gathering made them not his, nothing else could. That *labour* put a distinction between them and common. That added something to them more than

---

[7] *Ibid.,* Par. 26, p. 328.

[8] *Ibid.,* Par. 27, pp. 328–29.

Nature, the common Mother of all, had done; and so they became his private right."[9]

Now, this account teaches us that property, and specifically private property, is not a social convention but must exist by nature, since each of us has an unavoidably private body or person, and must appropriate things to its use in order to live. But from this point on Locke's chapter on property presents two contrary teachings. On the surface Locke, quoting the Bible, suggests something like this: God has given us all things richly. And in the state of nature there is a natural limit to what any individual may "ingross." The natural limit is the result of the fact that all the things useful for bodily survival—food and drink, etc.—can *spoil*. "As much as anyone can make use of to any advantage of life before its spoils; so much he may by his labour fix a Property in. Whatever is beyond this, is more than his share, and belongs to others. Nothing was made by God for Man to spoil or destroy. And thus considering the plenty of natural Provisions there was a long time in the World, and the few spenders, and to how small a part of that provision the industry of one Man could extend it self, and ingross it to the prejudice of others; especially keeping within the *bounds*, set by reason of what might serve for his *use*; there could be then little room for Quarrels or Contentions about Property so establish'd."[10]

---

[9] *Ibid.,* Par. 28, pp. 329-30.

[10] *Ibid.,* Par. 31, p. 332.

This stable and apparently pleasant state of affairs, Locke suggests, must have lasted until the invention of money. Money, which does not spoil, allowed men to ingross more than they needed—thus leading to shortages and scarcity, want, and eventually quarrels and enmity. "This is certain," Locke continues, "That in the beginning, before the desire of having more than Men needed, had altered the intrinsick value of things, which depends only on their usefulness to the Life of Man; or Men had *agreed, that a little piece of yellow Metal*, which would keep without wasting or decay, should be worth a great piece of Flesh, or a whole heap of Corn; though Men had a right to appropriate, by their Labour, each one to himself, as much of the things of Nature, as he could use: Yet this could not be much, nor to the Prejudice of others, where the same plenty was still left, to those who would use the same Industry."[11] This account then seems to accord with the traditional Christian view that love of money is the root of all evil, and to suggest that except for the unfortunate development of a social convention, namely, that "a little piece of yellow metal" is worth much of nature's plenty, men would have been well off indeed.

But Locke means for the careful reader to see something else here. What had God or nature given us richly?

[11] *Ibid.*, Par. 37, pp. 335-36.

Land, Locke answers, and proceeds to show that land—as we receive it from God or nature—is worthless. Our natural condition is not one of plenty but of desperate poverty, a hand-to-mouth existence where men are subject to death and starvation with the least misfortune. "God, when he gave the World in common to all Mankind, commanded Man also to labour, and the penury of his Condition required it of him."[12] It is man's labour, Locke says, that "*makes the far greatest part of the value of things,* we enjoy in this World: And the ground which produces the materials, is scarce to be reckon'd in, as any, or at most, but a very small, part of it; So little, that even amongst us, Land that is left wholly to Nature, that hath no improvement of Pasturage, Tillage, or Planting, is called, as indeed it is, wast; and we shall find the benefit of it amount to little more than nothing."[13]

And this leads us to view things in quite a different light. The natural limit to appropriation, which results from spoilage, is better viewed as a constraint, because it places a kind of ceiling on men's industriousness or energy. Why expend more effort than is needed to live hand to mouth, since things will spoil before they can be consumed? As Locke puts it, "Where there is not something both lasting and scarce, and so valuable to be

[12] *Ibid.*, Par. 32, p. 332.
[13] *Ibid.*, Par. 42, p. 339.

hoarded up, there Men will not be apt to enlarge their *Possessions of Land*, were it never so rich, never so free for them to take."[14] Money, then, is not the cause of man's troubles of scarcity and contention. Rather, scarcity, want, and contention are man's natural lot until the invention of money liberates human industriousness, allows men to work hard and accumulate wealth, and thus improve the lot of all. "He who appropriates land to himself by his labour, does not lessen but increase the common stock of mankind."[15]

Locke's deeper teaching about property, then, contradicts what the casual reader is likely to see. Private property is natural, according to Locke, but "the penury of man's condition" means there is no idyllic state of nature where men live a life of ease. Wealth is almost wholly the product of human labor (Locke says 999/1000 of the value of things is the result of labor). What prevents most human beings, in most times and places, from having wealth and security is that without appropriate conventions (such as money, but also laws and civil society), they have neither opportunity nor incentive to apply themselves energetically to the generation of prosperity. Wealth is generated, not found, and consists of human energy and ability.

This compelling account was to have great long-term

[14] *Ibid.,* Par. 48, p. 343.
[15] *Ibid.,* Par. 37, p. 336.

significance, as will be seen later in considering the ideas
of Adam Smith. Locke was perhaps the first great thinker
to grasp the rudiments of modern liberal economics, and
to incorporate a radically new understanding of wealth
into his political philosophy. He argued that the preservation of property—meaning men's "lives, liberties and
estates"—is the basic justification for all civil order. "The
great and *chief end*, therefore, of Men's uniting into com-
monwealths, and putting themselves under Government,
is the *Preservation of their Property*."[16] The state of nature is
deficient, Locke says, because men lack "an *established*, settled, known *Law*," and they also lack "a known and indif-
ferent Judge, with Authority to determine all differences
according to the established Law."[17] These notions of an
independent judiciary and the rule of law (rather than the
decrees of a chieftain) have already been seen as cardinal
principles of the English understanding of civil order as
England emerged from the Middle Ages. One could say
that Locke supplied the theoretical foundation for emerging English practices.

According to Locke, by thinking about man's natural
condition we can see clearly the basis of civil order or
"political society." He argues: "Men being, as has been
said, by Nature, all free, equal and independent, no one

[16] *Ibid.,* Par. 124, p. 395.
[17] *Ibid.,* Par. 125, p. 396.

can be put out of this Estate, and subjected to the Political Power of another, without his own *Consent*. The only way whereby any one devests himself of his Natural Liberty, and *puts on the bonds of Civil Society* is by agreeing with other Men to joyn and unite into a Community, for their comfortable, safe, and peaceable living one amongst another, in a secure Enjoyment of their Properties, and a greater Security against any that are not of it."[18] Moreover, no society not constituted in this way can be considered legitimate. "And thus that, which begins and actually *constitutes any Political Society*, is nothing but the consent of any number of Freemen capable of a majority to unite and incorporate into such a Society. And this is that, and that only, which did, or could give *beginning* to any *lawful Government* in the World."[19] This is of course a shocking assertion, since it raises questions about the legitimacy of many actual societies, as Locke's contemporaries were well aware.

Locke anticipates the reader asking a different question: How—since men are almost always born *into* an existing civil society—can they be said to have a choice? Locke's answer has a profound importance for us today. No man can give consent to a political society on behalf of anyone else, including his own son or daughter: if that were pos-

[18] *Ibid.*, Par. 95, pp. 375-76.
[19] *Ibid.*, Par. 99, p. 377.

sible, Locke admits, we could truly be said to be born into subjection to the laws of a commonwealth to which we had not consented. Rather, he says, each man or woman is born free, and becomes a member of a commonwealth by agreeing to accept its protections. Most commonly this is done by what Locke calls "tacit consent." "Nobody doubts," Locke says, "but an *express Consent*, of any Man entering into any Society, makes him a perfect Member of that Society, a Subject of that Government. The difficulty is, what ought to be look'd upon as a *tacit Consent*, and how far it binds, i.e., how far any one shall be looked on to have consented, and thereby submitted to any Government, when he has made no Expressions of it at all. And to this I say, that every Man, that hath any Possession, or Enjoyment, of any part of the Dominions of any Government, doth thereby give his tacit Consent, and is as far forth obliged to obedience to the Laws of that Government, during such Enjoyment, as anyone under it."[20] From this we can see that no commonwealth can claim the legitimate consent of its members unless they are free to leave the commonwealth: any society that denies the *right of emigration* undermines its own legitimacy.

Several other features of Locke's account of civil society deserve our attention. Locke is less concerned than was Hobbes about the dangers of civil war, which accord-

[20] *Ibid.,* Par. 119, p. 392.

ing to Hobbes meant that a powerful sovereign is best. Locke worries more about the possibility of an oppressive government, and so insists on the necessity of *limiting* the sovereign power as much as possible. According to Locke, the "Supream power" of any commonwealth is the legislative power, but even this power must not be arbitrary. It may not, for example, "*take* from any man any part of his *Property* without his own consent. For the preservation of Property being the end of Government, and that for which Men enter into Society, it necessarily supposes and requires, that the People should have Property, without which they must be suppos'd to lose that by entring into Society, which was the end for which they entered into it, too gross an absurdity for any Man to own."[21] The sovereign power must govern, first by "*promulgated establish'd Laws*, not to be varied in particular Cases, but to have one Rule for Rich and Poor, for the Favourite at Court, and the Country Man at Plough."[22] These notions are summed up in the phrase "popular sovereignty."

Locke insists on one final limitation of the power of government as a protection against tyranny. Though the legislative is the supreme power, he writes, "yet the Legislative being only a Fiduciary Power to act for certain ends, there remains *still in the People a Supream Power* to

[21] *Ibid.*, Par. 138, p. 406.
[22] *Ibid.*, Par. 142, p. 409.

remove or *alter the Legislative,* when they find the *Legislative* to act contrary to the trust reported in them."[23] This he calls, in fact, the "best fence against rebellion," because the existence of this principle should put rulers on notice that they are ultimately responsible to the people they govern. It is no accident that Locke's principles were widely understood to justify England's Glorious Revolution in 1688, in which King James II was forced to abdicate the throne and flee to France, to be replaced by a ruler more congenial to the English people. And a distant echo of this Lockean notion can be noted in the American Declaration of Independence a century later:

> We hold these Truths to be self-evident, that all Men are created equal, that they are endowed by their Creator with certain unalienable Rights, that among these are Life, Liberty and the Pursuit of Happiness. —That to secure these Rights, Governments are instituted among Men, deriving their just Powers from the Consent of the Governed, that whenever any Form of Government becomes destructive to these Ends, it is the Right of the People to alter or to abolish it, and to institute new Government, laying its Foundation on such Principles and organizing its Powers in such Form, as to them shall seem most likely to effect their Safety and Happiness.

---

[23] *Ibid.,* Par. 149, p. 413.

Chapter 9

COMMERCE AND LIBERTY

John Locke's profound teaching about the nature of man and the basis of legitimate political order is the clearest articulation of the principles of liberal individualism. He taught that human beings confront a nature that, left to itself, offers only scarcity, want, and insecurity. Human beings can escape this condition only by yielding some of their limitless but insecure rights by a social contract to live in a community under law, which makes it possible for them to preserve themselves, secure their genuine liberties, and produce the material goods needed for life, all of which Locke calls "property." In many of these principles Locke followed earlier thinkers such as Thomas Hobbes, but unlike Hobbes, Locke was deeply concerned about the power of the government itself. Governments are legitimate only if they rest on the consent of the people, according to Locke. But this principle alone is not enough. Men need to secure their liberties against all centers of power, and that includes the government itself.

Locke's teaching anticipated the slogan that "eternal vigilance is the price of liberty," for he believed the best safeguard against oppressive or tyrannical rulers is a citizenry educated to understand their rights and the principles of legitimate government, and aware of their "right of rebellion" in case tyrannical rule exceeds its proper bounds. In fact, he maintained that the right of rebellion is itself "the best fence against rebellion." Locke insisted that the instability that may result from such a doctrine cannot ever be avoided: "This is *an Inconvenience,* I confess, *that attends all Governments* whatsoever, when the Governours have brought it to this pass, to be generally suspected of their People; the most dangerous state which they can possibly put themselves in; wherein they are the less to be pitied, because it is so easie to be avoided; It being as impossible for a Governour, if he really means the good of his People, and the preservation of them, and their Laws together, not to make them see and feel it, as it is for the Father of a Family, not to let his Children see he loves, and takes care of them."[1]

One of the clearest statements of Locke's understanding of government is found in the concluding chapter of his *Second Treatise*: "The Reason why Men enter into

---

[1] Locke, *Second Treatise*, Par. 209, p. 453.

Society, is the preservation of their Property; and the end why they chuse and authorize a Legislative, is, that there may be Laws made, and Rules set, as Guards and Fences to the Properties of all the Members of the Society, to limit the Power, and moderate the Dominion, of every Part and Member of the Society."[2]

An additional means of protecting against "arbitrary or excessive" power was suggested by Locke's great successor, the French philosopher Charles Secondat, Baron de Montesquieu. Montesquieu is best known for his remarkable study, *Spirit of the Laws* (*Esprit des Lois*), the most famous part of which is his teaching about the separation of powers. "Separation of powers" refers to the idea that any legitimate political government must perform three functions, and that responsibility for each is best kept in separate hands in order to protect against tyranny. Any nonarbitrary government governs by laws, rather than arbitrary decrees or diktats. The core of political rule is the formulation of the laws themselves, which is the function of a legislature in the best case (Montesquieu's model was the British Parliament). But the application and enforcement of laws is an *executive* function; and this duty, along with the conduct of foreign policy (which requires energy, secrecy, and dispatch), is the proper function of a branch of government *separate* from the legislative. Finally,

[2] *Ibid.*, Par. 222, p. 460.

any political society must have a means of resolving disputes, which may arise under the laws, and which require
that the laws be interpreted carefully and applied fairly.
This is the role of the judicial branch, and in a well-organ-
ized government the judiciary should be as independent
as possible of both the legislative and executive
branches—especially since the courts will, in all criminal
cases, be hearing charges brought against citizens by an
arm of the executive branch (police powers being an
executive function).

Separation of powers is thus an important part of the
theory of modern liberal societies based on individual
rights. But we must consider a vexing question. By what
name should societies of this type be known? Often today
we call them "liberal democracies," but for a number of
reasons this is confusing. First, neither in the theories nor
in the practical examples of this kind of society did genuine democracy play much of a role in the eighteenth
century, or since. The greatest example of the kind of
regime we mean in those days was England, which was, of
course, a monarchical society. To be sure, it had a
Parliament, and to be sure, one of the cardinal principles
of Locke's political philosophy was "Popular Sovereignty."
But Locke did not mean democracy—actual government
by "the people"; he meant rather that the sovereignty ultimately belongs to all parties to the social contract, and also
that a government is formed, and powers delegated to it,

to rule and make decisions on practical matters. A better term to describe the sort of society Locke preferred is "commercial republic." The word "republic" indicates the complex balance of various elements—including, in England, social classes, such as king, lords, and commons—which make up the society. And "commercial" distinguishes this type of republic from its ancient antecedent, the classical republic, the most famous examples of which were Rome and Sparta. And this leads us to a very interesting controversy.

This eighteenth-century controversy can explain something about the politics of liberal commercial societies today. The last half century has seen much argument, in Western Europe and the United States, about the decency and desirability of liberal individualism. Those on the Right, including most famously Aleksandr Solzhenitsyn, accuse these societies of having sacrificed too much to the pursuit of wealth and prosperity, and lost their virtues—especially courage—in the process. The even more common accusations from the political Left hold that excessive and vulgar individualism has eroded the sense of community by emphasizing selfishness at the expense of sympathy and charity for others. Without the willingness of citizens to sacrifice for the community as a whole, they complain, liberal individualist societies are only collections of selfish atoms with no public spirit. Without public spirit and a sense of community, it is argued, such societies cannot satisfy the deepest human needs and perhaps cannot long survive.

The controversy sounds eerily familiar to anyone familiar with eighteenth-century political thought. Soon after Locke and Montesquieu had articulated the principles of liberal societies, others began to complain, in terms that anticipated closely the charges leveled today against liberal commercial societies. Eighteenth-century spokesmen for traditional institutions—above all the Church and the monarchy—deplored the new commercial way of life, which they saw as a threat to the old hierarchical ordering of English society. Free individuals pursuing commercial activities, after all, did disrupt the old order where everyone knew his place and stayed in it. At the same time other theorists, most notably the famous French thinker Jean-Jacques Rousseau, attacked the emerging commercial republican way of life for alienating men from their true needs and deepest attachments.

Rousseau's *Discourse on the Arts and Sciences* assailed the very notion of moral and scientific progress, and held up the ancient republic as a model for social order. In Rousseau's words, "Ancient politicians incessantly talked about morals and virtue, those of our time talk only of business and money."[3] According to Rousseau, the ancient

---

[3] Jean-Jacques Rousseau, *Discourse on the Sciences and Arts (First Discourse)*, translated by Judith R. Masters and edited by Roger Masters (New York: St. Martin's Press, 1964), p. 51.

republics were superior because they were dedicated to virtue, and though they were poor materially, their citizens willingly sacrificed their own happiness to the public good. Progress in the arts and sciences, far from freeing men and women and making their lives better, according to Rousseau, only makes them more dependent on each other and hence enslaves them to social customs and the good opinion of others. "Civilized peoples," according to Rousseau, are "happy slaves," who have "the semblance of all the virtues without the possession of any."[4] The simple and ignorant way of life of ancient republics is to be preferred, according to Rousseau, because human beings are happiest and most independent when their needs are few and easily met. "Behold," he wrote, "how luxury, licentiousness, and slavery have in all periods been punishment for the arrogant attempts we have made to emerge from the happy ignorance in which eternal wisdom has placed us."[5]

The attacks on commerce and luxury, then, played a large role in the debates about emerging liberal individualist society. The chief sides in the controversy came to be identified with two kinds of republics: the large modern commercial republic, praised by Montesquieu, and the small ancient republic, symbolized by Rome and Sparta. Partisans of each way of life were forced to defend against

[4] *Ibid.*, p. 36.
[5] *Ibid.*, p. 46.

the arguments advanced by the other side.

One of these two outlooks eventually carried the day in the eighteenth century, in practice if not in theory, even though its counterpart continued to attract adherents for many decades, and has had periodic resurgences over the last two centuries—resurgences that seem to coincide with times when the other view is having practical difficulties and is unable to defend itself persuasively. The victorious side is that of the large modern commercial republic. But the partisans of the ancient republic have never ceased to offer an alternative attractive to some. The terms of the controversy are instructive.

The most important defenders of the large modern commercial republic, interestingly enough, came from a relatively backward nation: they were the great thinkers of the Scottish Enlightenment, above all David Hume and Adam Smith. Since Smith will be the subject of another chapter, the focus here is on David Hume's decisive contribution to what might be called the controversy over commercial republics.

Hume was a near contemporary of Baron Montesquieu, and in fact they corresponded with each other. Hume admired *Spirit of the Laws*, and no doubt learned from it. Though Montesquieu is sometimes read as a defender of ancient republics, which he said have *virtue* as their main animating principle, a careful reading elicits the subtle suggestion that perhaps these ancient republics demanded too much from human nature. For in order to focus all the energies of citizens on public goals, they too frequently resorted either to religious fanaticism or to war and conquest as national goals. In a chapter entitled "What virtue is in the political state," he compares the virtuous republic to monastic life: "Why do monks love so much their order? Their love comes from the same thing that makes their order intolerable to them. Their rule deprives them of everything upon which ordinary passions rest; what remains, therefore, is the passion for the very rule that afflicts them. The more austere it is, that is, the more it curtails their inclinations, the more force it gives to those that remain."[6]

Hume shared both Montesquieu's interest in and deep learning about the history of republics. And he set out to show, in plain and simple terms, that the costs exacted by the ancient participatory republics were much greater than their partisans understood. He tackled head-on the nostalgia for ancient manners and politics, suggesting it was only an example of the too common human tendency to venerate the past and denigrate the present. But above all he showed that the ancient republics invariably depended on cruel and oppressive systems of slavery, from which their modern champions always averted their eyes.

The clearest expression of Hume's carefully thought

---

[6] Montesquieu, *The Spirit of the Laws* (Cambridge: Cambridge University Press, 1989), Bk. 5, Ch. 2, p. 43.

out views on republics is found in his political *Essays*. The longest of these, in fact, is devoted to the question of the relative populousness of ancient and modern nations. This is important because it was universally understood—by Hume and his opponents—that greater populousness is a sign of a healthy political or civic order. The champions of ancient republics believed that the populations of modern nations (1750) were smaller than those of their ancient predecessors; Hume set out to prove the contrary. In addition to being an impressive exercise in demographics, Hume's essay offers powerful arguments on the direct superiority of modern republican organization. Here is a sample:

> The chief difference between the domestic economy of the ancients and that of the moderns consists in the practice of slavery, which prevailed among the former, and which has been abolished for some centuries throughout the greater part of Europe. Some passionate admirers of the ancients, and zealous partizans of civil liberty, (for these sentiments, as they are, both of them, in the main, extremely just, are found to be almost inseparable) cannot forbear regretting the loss of this institution; and whilst they brand all submission to the government of a single person with the harsh denomination of slavery, they would gladly reduce the greater part of mankind to real slavery and subjection. But to one who considers coolly on the subject it will appear, that human nature, in gen-

eral, really enjoys more liberty at present, in the most arbitrary government of Europe, than it ever did during the
most flourishing period of ancient times.[7]

In his famous essays on political economy Hume was
even more direct. He admitted that the ancient nations
emphasized public spiritedness, and indeed sacrificed the
happiness of individual citizens to the national or public
interest.

> It is natural on this occasion to ask, whether sovereigns
> may not return to the maxims of ancient policy, and con-
> sult their own interest in this respect, more than the hap-
> piness of their subjects? I answer, that it appears to me,
> almost impossible; and that because ancient policy was
> violent, and contrary to the more natural and usual course
> of things. It is well known with what peculiar laws Sparta
> was governed, and what a prodigy that republic is justly
> esteemed by every one who has considered human nature
> as it has displayed itself in other nations, and other ages.
> Were the testimony of history less positive and circum-
> stantial, such a government would appear a mere philo-
> sophical whim or fiction, and impossible ever to be
> reduced to practice. And though the Roman and other
> ancient republics were supported on principles somewhat
> more natural, yet was there an extraordinary concurrence

[7] David Hume, *Essays*, edited by Eugene Miller (Indianapolis: Liberty Classics,
1985), p. 383.

of circumstances to make them submit to such grievous burthens. They were free states; they were small ones; and the age being martial, all their neighbors were continually in arms. Freedom naturally begets public spirit, especially in small states; and this public spirit, this *amor patriae*, must encrease, when the public is almost in continual alarm, and men are obliged, every moment, to expose themselves to the greatest dangers for its defence. A continual succession of wars makes every citizen a soldier; He takes the field in his turn: And during his service he is chiefly maintained by himself. This service is indeed equivalent to a heavy tax; yet is it less felt by a people addicted to arms, who fight for honour and revenge more than pay, and are unacquainted with gain and industry as well as pleasure.[8]

Now, what this all adds up to is a spirited and lucid defense of liberal commercial republics—where individuals chiefly pursue security and prosperity, for themselves and their families, while the state or government aims only to ensure the peaceful and lawful conditions for individuals to flourish as they choose—against the ancient republics devoted to virtue and demanding enormous individual sacrifice. Recall Thomas Hobbes's teaching that it was precisely the ancient republic's pursuit of virtue—about which nations disagree—that engendered bloody

[8] *Ibid.,* pp. 258-59.

wars and fierce competition and made peace and prosperity impossible. The liberal commercial order has always
been bound up with the notion that politics should be
concerned not with virtue or salvation but with peace
and prosperity, bodily needs on which all human beings—
whatever their vision of heaven or the lack of it—can
agree.

Chapter 10

WEALTH, COOPERATION, AND FREEDOM

We turn now to another great figure of the Scottish Enlightenment, Adam Smith, author of the famous *Inquiry into the Nature and Causes of the Wealth of Nations*. In this classic work Smith articulated the basic principles of what we know today as free market or free enterprise capitalism. What does capitalism have to do with liberal individualism or liberal societies generally? And why should Adam Smith be identified with capitalism—a word he never used and one he probably would not have approved? Briefly: what we think of today as capitalism has as its central principle the notion of the free movement of all economic resources, which means in turn the reliance on private ownership of property so that resource allocation is completely decentralized, as free as possible of all government control. Thus capitalism entails the notion of a minimal role for the state, just as John Locke had suggested: the reason each man submits to government is, as Locke puts it, "the better to preserve himself, his Liberty and Property," which requires "known and settled laws," "known authoris'd judges," and strict limits on arbitrary power. Adam Smith gives a detailed account of why such an arrangement best promotes what Locke saw as the only valid goal of a legitimate political order.

Smith began his investigation with a plain question, though not an easy one. What, he wanted to know, explains the large disparity between relatively wealthy nations and poor ones? What *is* wealth and what makes us consider a nation wealthy? Even his title reveals a crucial presupposition, namely, that the conditions involved in producing wealth are *political* conditions, since they have to do with nations—the political entities that set peoples apart from one another. Smith knew of course that there are wealthy and poor individuals in many societies, but he was intrigued by the fact that in what he called a "civilized" nation even "the very meanest person" lives with relative security and ease compared to someone in a primitive society. "The accommodation of an European prince," he wrote, "does not always so much exceed that of an industrious and frugal peasant, as the accommodation of the latter exceeds that of many an African king, the absolute master of the lives and liberties of ten thousand naked savages."[1] This agrees with Locke's demonstration

[1] Adam Smith, *An Inquiry into the Nature and Causes of the Wealth of Nations* (Indianapolis: Liberty Classics, 1976), I. i.11. (Book I, chapter 1, paragraph 11), p. 24.

that by nature human beings live a hand-to-mouth existence, in conditions of "penury" and want. Wealth, in
other words, is not a natural commodity that only needs
to be distributed, but something human beings produce.
And wealth does not consist in "natural resources." Just as
Locke had said, it is human labor that makes things useful
and valuable to us.

How is wealth generated? Smith began from a simple
observation:

> The annual labour of every nation is the fund that origi-
> nally supplies it with all the necessaries and conveniencies
> of life, which it annually consumes, and which consist
> always either in the immediate produce of that labour, or
> in what is purchased with that produce from other
> nations.
>
> According, therefore, as this produce, or what is pur-
> chased with it, bears a greater or smaller proportion to the
> number of those who are to consume it, the nation will
> be better or worse supplied with all the necessaries and
> conveniences for which it has occasion.[2]

Now, Smith observes, this proportion depends on two
circumstances. One is the "skill, dexterity, and judgment"
with which labor is applied. The other is the ratio of
industrious or productive people to the idle, that is, to
those not engaged in productive work. The first of these
variables, Smith teaches, is by far the more important:

[2] *Ibid.,* I.intro.2, p. 10.

Among the savage nations of hunters and fishers, every individual who is able to work, is more or less employed in useful labour, and endeavors to provide, as well as he can, the necessaries and conveniencies of life, for himself, or such of his family or tribe as are either too old, or too young, or too infirm to go a hunting and fishing. Such nations, however, are so miserably poor, that, from mere want, they are frequently reduced, or, at least, think themselves reduced, to the necessity sometimes of directly destroying, and sometimes of abandoning their infants, their old people, and those afflicted with lingering diseases, to perish with hunger, or to be devoured by wild beasts. Among civilized and thriving nations, on the contrary, though a great number of people do not labour at all, many of whom consume the produce of ten times, frequently of a hundred times more labour than the greater part of those who work; yet the produce of the whole labour of the society is so great, that all are often abundantly supplied, and a workman, even of the lowest and poorest order, if he is frugal and industrious, may enjoy a greater share of the necessaries and conveniences of life than it is possible for any savage to acquire."[3]

The focus in the first part of the *Wealth of the Nations* is on the ways in which improvements occur in the "skill, dexterity, and judgment" with which labor is applied. And

---

[3] *Ibid.,* I.intro.4, p. 10.

his analysis led Smith to conclude that the most important factor in their improvement is one thing: the division of labor. He described the fantastic improvement in productive power that results from specialization. This is so obvious today that it is rarely mentioned, but Smith illustrated his point with a now-famous example of a pin factory. He observed that "a workman not educated to this business," nor acquainted with the use of the machinery employed in it, "could scarce, perhaps, with his utmost industry, make one pin in a day, and certainly could not make twenty."[4] But with specialization, and the machinery to which it gives rise, ten workers in a pin factory can easily produce "upwards of forty-eight thousand pins in a day"—a staggering productivity increase per capita. Thus by the division of labor each of us can become hundreds or thousands of times more productive, compared to what we could be if each had to provide everything for himself.

What fascinated Smith was the principle underlying this possibility, and in particular the very great interdependence that must exist in a society where specialization is extensive. Each individual in a commercial economy is dependent on a vast number of others for the satisfaction of his needs. How is cooperation on such a scale possible? And how can any individual have a reasonable expectation that his needs or wants will be fulfilled? What leads

[4] *Ibid.,* I.i.3, p. 14.

each individual to specialize in something that will be in demand? To take the last question first, Smith examined a traditional assumption, going back at least to Plato, that individuals specialize in different activities because each person's natural talents and abilities are suited to different tasks. Adam Smith did not believe this persuasive, for he thought people much more equal in their abilities, potentially at least. "The difference of natural talents," he said, "in different men is, in reality, much less than we are aware of; and the very different genius which appears to distinguish men of different professions, when grown up to maturity, is not upon many occasions so much the cause as the effect of the division of labour. The difference between the most dissimilar characters, between a philosopher and a common street porter, for example, seems to arise not so much from nature as from habit, custom, and education."[5]

This example suggests that environmental factors, as we say today, are much more influential than the older view admitted. Without the division of labor—which arises from a natural "propensity to truck, barter, and exchange" unique to human beings—"every man must have procured to himself every necessary and conveniency of life which he wanted. All must have had the same duties to perform, and the same work to do, and there could have

[5] *Ibid.*, I.ii.4, p. 28.

been no such difference of employment as could alone give occasion to any great difference of talents."[6] This is roughly the way in which all animals of the same species are equal—each animal must provide what it needs to survive or else it does not survive. According to Smith it is precisely this rough equality of capacities that allows men to specialize to the benefit of others.

The "propensity to truck, barter, and exchange one thing for another" is crucial to answering another of Smith's fundamental questions, how such an amazing degree of cooperation as exists in a commercial society can develop without coercion or government direction. The propensity to trade or exchange is "common to all men, and to be found in no other race of animals, which seem to know neither this nor another species of contracts."[7] As Smith illustrates it, "Nobody ever saw a dog make a fair and deliberate exchange of one bone for another with another dog. Nobody ever saw one animal by its gestures and natural cries signify to another, this is mine, that yours; I am willing to give this for that. When an animal wants to obtain something either of a man or of another animal, it has no other means of persuasion but to gain the favor of those whose service it requires. A puppy fawns upon its dam, and a spaniel endeavors by a

---

[6] *Ibid.,* I.ii.4, p. 29.

[7] *Ibid.,* I.ii.2, p. 25.

thousand attractions to engage the attention of its master who is at dinner, when it wants to be fed by him."[8] Smith notes that a man may sometimes depend on begging, or claims of need alone, for the satisfaction of his wants, but unless he is desperately poor and his needs few, no man can live entirely by begging. "In civilized society he stands at all times in need of the co-operation and assistance of great multitudes, while his whole life is scarce sufficient to gain the friendship of a few persons. In almost every other race of animals each individual, when it is grown up to maturity, is entirely independent, and in its natural state has occasion for the assistance of no other living creature. But man has almost constant occasion for the help of his brethren, and it is in vain for him to expect it from their benevolence only."[9]

And this led Smith to the insight for which he is perhaps most famous: almost no one wants to depend entirely on the benevolence of others. "He will be more likely to prevail if he can interest their self-love in his favour, and show them that it is for their own advantage to do for him what he requires of them."[10] This is the key to understanding how we can depend on and cooperate with many others, yet do so voluntarily. "Whoever offers to

---

[8] *Ibid.*, I.ii.2, p. 26.

[9] *Ibid.*

[10] *Ibid.*, I.ii.2, p. 27.

another a bargain of any kind, proposes to do this," Smith
states. "Give me that which I want, and you shall have this
which you want, is the meaning of every such offer; and
it is in this manner that we obtain from one another the
far greater part of those good offices which we stand in
need of. It is not from the benevolence of the butcher, the
brewer, or the baker, that we expect our dinner, but from
their regard to their own interest. We address ourselves,
not to their humanity but to their self-love, and never talk
to them of our own necessities but of their advantages."[11]

If the division of labor arises from natural human inclinations, and allows us to overcome the want and scarcity
to which all nations can trace their history, why are not all
nations equally wealthy? Why do they not all enjoy the
benefits of an extensive division of labor? What limits the
specialization that makes men and women so much more
productive? Though a number of factors emerge in the
course of Smith's analysis, the clearest statement comes
quite early: the division of labor is limited by the size of
the market. As Smith puts it, "When the market is very
small, no person can have any encouragement to dedicate
himself entirely to one employment, for want of the
power to exchange all that surplus part of the produce of
his own labour, which is over and above his own con-
sumption, for such parts of the produce of other men's

---

[11] *Ibid.,* I.ii.2, pp. 26-27.

labour as he has occasion for."[12] This means that ease of transportation and technological development—itself the result of division of labor—make possible a more extensive market for trade, and thus more specialization. A pin factory—with its production of 48,000 pins a day— cannot exist in a small village that cannot trade its surplus in a larger market. But size of market implicitly includes many other things—for example, ease of exchange, which requires some form of money. The pin maker would have no way to obtain bread if the baker did not use or need pins, unless there were some commodity both easy to transport and acceptable to all as a medium of exchange. Thus Smith enters into a lengthy examination of the concept of money.

Two things are important in this discussion of money. First, Smith stresses again and again that wealth does not consist in money. Money is only a medium of exchange, used to measure the value of goods or labor, but wealth consists in productive abilities or, in some cases, of stored up labor in the form of tools or stock. Think of an extreme case: a pocket full of money, or a bank account with a high balance, do not make someone wealthy if he cannot buy the things or services he wishes to obtain. The confusion of wealth with money—even in one of its most common forms, gold—was the root of the great fallacy of

[12] *Ibid.,* I.iii.1, p. 31.

mercantilism, as Smith showed. Mercantilism induced nations to seek to accumulate gold, even to the extent of banning trade in some cases, thus thwarting the development of their productive capacity, which would truly have made them wealthy.

Smith also points out that, though money is related to the value of things, there are two senses of value, and economics as a science is concerned with only one of these. "The word VALUE, it is to be observed," he says, "has two different meanings, and sometimes expresses the utility of some particular object, and sometimes the power of purchasing other goods which the possession of that object conveys. The one may be called 'value in use' the other, 'value in exchange.' The things which have the greatest value in use have frequently little or no value in exchange; and on the contrary, those which have the greatest value in exchange have frequently little or no value in use. Nothing is more useful than water; but it will purchase scarce any thing; scarce any thing can be had in exchange for it. A diamond, on the contrary, has scarce any value in use; but a very great quantity of other goods may frequently be had in exchange for it."[13] The exchange-value (as Marx later called it) of something leads Smith to a discussion of price, the heart of any account of free-market economics. This discussion has most relevance today for

[13] *Ibid.*, I.iv.13, pp.44–45.

those interested in the difference between free-market economies and the "command economies" of the former communist system. We will consider Smith's account of price, and the way free markets allocate resources, in the next chapter.

Chapter 11

PRICES AND MARKETS

Smith demonstrated that the wealth of a nation consists in its productive capacity, or in the "skill, dexterity, and judgment" with which the total fund of its labor is applied. Labor, of course, includes all forms of productive activity, intellectual and physical, and takes into account tools, machinery, and so on, which multiply productive capacity. In any developed economy, or "civilized society" as Smith called it, there is a very great degree of interdependence because the division of labor is so extensive, and Smith offered a convincing account of how it is possible for large numbers of individuals to cooperate with and depend on each other without having to be commanded or directed. To see how this is possible in a liberal commercial society, it is best to follow Smith's investigation of the concept of price.

Although it seems simple, the concept of price is actually quite complex. Smith helps us grasp its essentials by distinguishing among several senses of price. The first distinction involves real and nominal price: though the nominal price of anything varies with the currency or measure in use, the "real price" is always the amount of effort required to produce the thing and bring it to market. In the simplest economies—which Smith asks us to think about in order to understand clearly—real price is almost entirely measured by the *time* required to produce an object. An arrow maker and a moccasin maker will exchange with each other based on an average day's work. "If among a nation of hunters, for example, it usually costs twice the labour to kill a beaver which it does to kill a deer," Smith explains, "one beaver should naturally exchange for or be worth two deer. It is natural that what is usually the produce of two days or two hours labour should be worth double of what is usually the produce of one day's or one hour's labour."[1]

As an economy develops and tools are used extensively, the cost of labor "stored up" in tools must also be taken into account. This is part of what Smith calls "stock," a term similar to what we today call "capital."

> As soon as stock has accumulated in the hands of particular persons, some of them will naturally employ it in setting to work industrious people, whom they will supply

---

[1] Smith, *Wealth of Nations* (I.vi.1), p. 30.

with materials, and subsistence, in order to make a profit by the sale of their work or by what their labour adds to the value of the materials. In exchanging the complete manufacture either for money, for labour, or for other goods, over and above what is sufficient to pay the price of the materials and the wages of the workmen, something must be given for the profits of the undertaker of the work who hazards his stock in this adventure. The value which the workmen add to the materials, therefore, resolves itself in this case into two parts, of which the one pays their wages, the other the profits of their employer upon the whole stock of materials and wages which he advanced. He could have no interest to employ them unless he expected from the sale of their work something more than what was sufficient to replace his stock to him; and he could have no interest to employ a great stock rather than a small one unless his profits were to bear some proportion to the extent of his stock.[2]

Likewise, when land is a factor in production, rent must be paid for its use. About this Smith is quite realistic, and we will see shortly why private ownership, even of land, makes a market more efficient.

As soon as the land of any country has all become private property, the landlords, like all other men, love to reap where they never sowed, and demand a rent even for its

[2] *Ibid.,* I.vi.5, pp. 65-66.

natural produce. The wood of the forest, the grass of the
field, and all the natural fruits of the earth, which when
land was in common, cost the labourer only the trouble
of gathering them, come, even to him, to have an additional price fixed upon them. He must give up to the
landlord a portion of what his labour either collects or
produces. This portion, or what comes to the same thing,
the price of this portion, constitutes the rent of land, and
in the price of the greater part of commodities makes a
third component part.[3]

All the factors that go into the cost of producing something must be figured into the total "effort" necessary to
bring it to market.

The most important distinction in Smith's analysis of
price—and the key to a free market—is that between natural price and market price. The natural price is what
every potential producer must think about before deciding whether to produce something. Smith points out, first,
that "there is in every society or neighborhood an ordinary or average rate both of wages and profit in every different employment of labour and stock."[4] He shows that
this rate is "naturally regulated. . .partly by the general circumstances of the society, their riches or poverty, their
advancing, stationary, or declining condition; and partly by

[3] *Ibid.,* I.vi.8, p. 67.
[4] *Ibid.,* I.vii.1, p. 72.

the particular nature of each employment."[5] The same
holds true for rent—every society or neighborhood has an
average or ordinary rent, depending on such factors as
natural or improved fertility, location, and so on. "These
ordinary or average rates may be called the natural rates of
wages, profit, and rent at the time and place in which they
commonly prevail. When the price of any commodity is
neither more nor less than what is sufficient to pay the
rent of the land, the wages of the labour, and the profits of
the stock employed in raising, preparing, and bringing it
to market, according to their natural rates, the commodity is then sold for what may be called its natural price."[6]

But the actual price at which a commodity sells is
independent of its natural price, for it depends on the
supply of and demand for the commodity. If there is an
oversupply of some good, its market price will fall, and
may fall below the price necessary to produce it—a signal
that an oversupply exists. This causes producers to redirect
their efforts toward some other good, where the market
price is higher than the natural price—a signal that more
of the commodity is being sought. In Smith's words,
"When the quantity of any commodity which is brought
to market falls short of the effectual demand, all those
who are willing to pay the whole value of the rent, wages,

[5] *Ibid.*
[6] *Ibid.,* I.vii.3-4, p. 72.

and profit, which must be paid in order to bring it thither, cannot be supplied with the quantity which they want. Rather than want it altogether, some of them will be willing to give more."[7] Smith concludes that "the natural price, therefore, is, as it were, the central price, to which the prices of all commodities are continually gravitating."[8] And as a result of this gravitational pull, "The whole quantity of industry annually employed in order to bring any commodity to market naturally suits itself in this manner to the effectual demand. It naturally aims at bringing always that precise quantity thither which may be sufficient to supply, and no more than supply, that demand."[9]

In a liberal commercial society each individual is presumed to be the best judge of his own interest, and is expected to decide, for example, on a career by considering all relevant factors—his own skills and aptitudes, the difficulty of training or education, the risk and rewards of this or that occupation, and so on. What about social needs? In a free market economy, the needs of society are automatically translated by the price mechanism into good pay for anyone filling the positions for which there is great demand. If engineers are in short supply, those who need engineers will have to bid up the "price" by

[7] *Ibid.,* I.vii.9, p. 73.

[8] *Ibid.,* IV.vii.15, p. 75.

[9] *Ibid.,* I.vii.16, p. 75.

competing for the engineers who are available. Young
people deciding on careers will be signaled by the high
pay of engineers—relative to other occupations of equal
difficulty and requiring equal training—and may decide
to enter that occupation. No one commands them to do
so, and any individual who would prefer, for example, to
be a musician, can do so, though an excess of skillful musi-
cians might have driven the price for their services down
so that the option may no longer seem attractive. Markets
continually signal, through prices, the needs and demands
of all participants in the economy. As Smith puts it:

> The whole of the advantages and disadvantages of the dif-
> ferent employments of labour and stock must, in the same
> neighbourhood, be either perfectly equal or continually
> tending to equality. If in the same neighbourhood, there
> was any employment evidently either more or less advan-
> tageous than the rest, so many people would crowd into it
> in the one case, and so many would desert it in the other,
> that its advantages would soon return to the level of other
> employments. This at least would be the case in a society
> where things were left to follow their natural course, where
> there was perfect liberty, and where every man was per-
> fectly free both to chuse what occupation he thought
> proper, and to change it as often as he thought proper.

Every man's interest would prompt him to seek the advantageous, and to shun the disadvantageous employment.[10]

A free market, then, guarantees that resources—not just
materials, but human energy, and tools, and inventive-
ness—will be directed into those endeavors where demand
or need is greatest, as signaled by the price mechanism
when market price exceeds natural price. As tastes and
needs change, resources are continually redirected. Free
market capitalism is thus a highly dynamic system, and as
long as prices are free and thousands of individuals control
resources—whether materials, land, or their own individual labor and energy—it is a system extremely sensitive to
the aggregate wants, needs, or desires of the society as a
whole. The market is a gigantic "allocation mechanism," as
economists like to say, for indicating where resources are
needed, where there are shortages and excesses.

Why does this depend on private ownership? It has
long been a delusion that planners can direct resources
where they are needed. Some even say individuals should
not make these decisions. But Smith believed individuals
are in general the best judges of their own needs and
wants, and even if they weren't, he believed it beyond the
capacity of *any* human mind or human wisdom to allocate
resources as efficiently as a free market can. Smith was
under no illusions as to the generosity of most men and

[10] *Ibid.,* I.x.1., p. 116

women. But a free market works automatically to channel individual efforts to the satisfaction of society's needs. "Every individual is continually exerting himself to find out the most advantageous employment for whatever capital he can command. It is his own advantage, indeed, and not that of the society, which he has in view. But the study of his own advantage naturally, or rather necessarily leads him to prefer that employment which is most advantageous to the society."[11] As Smith puts it in a famous passage, the individual may labor only to make the most of his own resources and intend only his own gain, but he "is led by an invisible hand to promote an end which was no part of his intention," namely, to maximize the satisfaction or utility for society as a whole. Smith adds an ironic comment: "By pursuing his own interest he frequently promotes that of the society more effectually than when he really intends to promote it. I have never known much good done by those who affected to trade for the publick good."[12]

Though free markets have proven most advantageous in practice for economic growth and prosperity, there are some special circumstances in which they do not work perfectly. These always involve some kind of "market externality," as economists call it, which means that some

[11] *Ibid.*, IV.ii.4, p. 454.
[12] *Ibid.*, IV.ii.9, p. 456.

cost (of production) or some benefit (as in the "product" produced) is for special reasons ignored—as, for example, when it isn't or can't be owned or bought or sold. The classic example is grazing on a village common—a pasture or plot of land that is owned by all, and that therefore is treated as a free good by the users (who pay no rent because there is no owner to collect it). This leads to over-grazing and thus ruination of the resource because each individual knows if he lets his sheep graze only a little bit (which he might do if the pasture were his own and he wanted to protect it for future use), others will use it up anyway, so he lets his sheep graze till the grass is uprooted. The solution to this problem of market failure is to *assign* ownership rights to the pasture, and let someone (i. e., a town council) charge rents for grazing there, using the price to regulate use so as to protect the pasture and max-imize output.

A similar problem has long been encountered in activ-ities where pollution of the environment occurs. Cleaning up pollution is properly a cost of production, but for a long time the cost was ignored, because it was easy for manufacturers (as one example) to pass the cost along to all others—in the form of dirty air or water—rather than only to purchasers of the product the manufacturer makes. This case of market failure can be corrected only by laws, which require that polluters pay the costs of cleaning up and then include the costs in their calculations of "natural price." This way the true cost of producing anything is reflected in price calculations. Sometimes this will redirect energies into alternative products or methods.

But for every case where some government intervention in a market is helpful to correct an externality, there are dozens of interventions requested by people who want to suppress competition and thus enjoy a subsidy. Smith warned that producers, landlords, and merchants will always attempt to enlist government help in ways that will maximize their gains by suppressing competition, either by granting monopolies, by prohibiting importation of foreign goods, or by other methods. But this is based on a misunderstanding called mercantilism, and unfortunately mercantilism is still common today. Smith explains:

> Consumption is the sole end and purpose of all production; and the interest of the producer ought to be attended to, only so far as it may be necessary for promoting that of the consumer. The maxim is so perfectly self-evident, that it would be absurd to attempt to prove it. But in the mercantile system, the interest of the consumer is almost constantly sacrificed to that of the producer; and it seems to consider production, and not consumption, as the ultimate end and object of all industry and commerce.[13]

---

[13] *Ibid.,* IV.viii.49, p. 660.

Governments are often inclined to interfere with what Smith called "the system of natural liberty," by promoting or hindering one industry or another. Any such government interference, however, "is in reality subversive of the great purpose which it means to promote. It retards, instead of accelerating, the progress of the society towards real wealth and greatness; and diminishes, instead of increasing, the real value of the annual produce of its land and labour."[14]

On this understanding we can see why Smith recommended a minimal role for government. "According to the system of natural liberty, the sovereign has only three duties to attend to; three duties of great importance, indeed, but plain and intelligible to common understandings."[15] The three duties of the government, according to Smith, are "first, the duty of protecting the society from the violence and invasion of other independent societies; secondly, the duty of protecting, as far as possible, every member of the society from the injustice or oppression of every other member of it, or the duty of establishing an exact administration of justice; and thirdly, the duty of erecting and maintaining certain publick works and certain publick institutions, which it can never be for the interest of any individual, or small number of individuals, to erect and maintain; because the profit could never repay

[14] *Ibid.,* IV.ix.50, p. 687.
[15] *Ibid.,* IV.ix.51, p. 687.

the expence to any individual or small number of individuals, though it may frequently do much more than repay it to a great society."[16] By public works he meant such things as lighthouses, or sometimes roads or bridges.

Even in so-called free market societies the last half century has witnessed an extraordinary growth of government activity and interference with market forces. More than a quarter of the wealth generated each year by individuals in the United States is now consumed by government, often in the conviction that it can be spent more wisely by bureaucrats. All such interference with free markets (trade protection, subsidies to particular industries or agricultural crops, etc.) distorts the market's ability to allocate resources efficiently. And the efficient allocation of all resources—land, tools, human ingenuity, raw materials, even time—is precisely what leads to prosperity, to the "wealth of nations." In socialist economies the figures are too depressing to recite. But Adam Smith—though aware of the tendency of governments to expand and interfere—offers us a note of hope: "The natural effort of every individual to better his own condition, when suffered to exert itself with freedom and security, is so powerful a principle, that it is alone, and without any assistance, not only capable of carrying on the society to wealth and prosperity, but of surmounting a hundred impertinent

[16] *Ibid.,* IV.ix.51, pp. 687-88.

obstructions with which the folly of human laws too often incumber its operations; though the effect of these obstructions is always more or less either to encroach upon its freedom, or to diminish its security."[17] Even today, and even in countries whose leaders should know better, this lesson is not firmly enough anchored in the minds of the political class.

[17] *Ibid.*, IV.v.b.43, p. 540.

Chapter 12

AMERICAN LIBERTY

The roots of liberal commercial society, as we have indi-
cated, can be traced almost entirely to the nations of
northwest Europe as they emerged from the Middle Ages.
And among these nations the leader, both in theory and
in practice, was England. There were other commercial
republics, most notably Holland, but only in England did
the historical practices—English common law, property
rights, a powerful Parliament checking the royal sovereign—combine with a theoretical understanding such as
was offered by John Locke to establish a basis for what was
known even in the eighteenth century as "English liberty." The Scotsman David Hume, in midcentury,
described the English constitution, after tracing its development over the source of many centuries, as "the most
perfect and most accurate system of liberty that was ever
found compatible with government."[1]

The disruptions of the English civil war and the sectarian strife of the seventeenth century had driven many
English subjects to flee their island in the hope of beginning life anew in the New World. It should be no surprise
that they took with them as much of the system of
English liberty as would survive the Atlantic crossing.
Indeed, in some respects their experiments in the New
World allowed English political practices to be tested in
conditions that revealed their strengths and weaknesses
with exceptional clarity. Some of the earliest settlers established among themselves civil compacts that anticipated
what Locke later called the "social contract." The most
famous of these is the "Mayflower Compact"—a political
covenant in which its framers "solemnly and mutually, in
the presence of God and one another, covenant and combine ourselves together into a civil body politic for our
better ordering and preservation, and furtherance of the
ends aforesaid."[2] It must immediately be added that these
communities were far from liberal, despite their view of
civil society is the result of a voluntary commitment by
individuals. Many of the Puritan settlements begun in
New England were virtual theocracies. Though communitarian, the Puritans saw themselves in Old Testament
terms as a chosen people of God.

[1] David Hume, *The History of England* (Indianapolis: Liberty Classics, 1983), Vol.
II, Ch. xxiii, p. 525.

[2] Mayflower Compact, in *The People Shall Judge*, p. 5.

New World settlements were out of necessity self-governing, since the secular powers that granted their charters
were thousands of miles distant. And the experience of
self-government recommended to them the wisdom and
utility of written compacts of constitutions, preparing the
way for perhaps the most important American contribution to self-governing liberal societies. But the thousands
of miles that separated England from the colonies were
among the causes of one of the most important political
events of recent centuries, namely, the American
Revolution.

Though it is tempting today to understand this event
in twentieth-century terms, as an early example of an
anticolonial libertarian struggle, to do so would be to mis-
understand its major significance. For the American rebellion against the British crown began not as an anticolonial
war but as an attempt to claim the very same English liberties just discussed. It was not a war against colonial rule
but against tyrannical rule, in the name of the right—not
merely of Englishmen but of all men—to government by
consent.

The most powerful statement of the Americans' understanding of what they were doing is, of course, found in
the famous Declaration of Independence, signed July 4,
1776. To those familiar with the foundations of liberal
society, this document is striking for its reliance on the
ideas and the very language of John Locke's great *Second*

Treatise of Civil Government. From the beginning, the American Revolution was informed by the deep reflections on human nature and politics of the whole tradition of liberal individualist thought in England and elsewhere. "We hold these truths to be self-evident," wrote Thomas Jefferson in the Declaration, "that all men are created equal, that they are endowed by their Creator with certain unalienable Rights, that among these are Life, Liberty, and the Pursuit of Happiness." This is Lockean enough, but the next sentences are pure Locke, even to the very words in places: "That to secure these Rights, Governments are instituted among Men, deriving their just Powers from the Consent of the Governed, that whenever any Form of Government becomes destructive of these Ends, it is the Right of the People to alter or abolish it, and to institute a new Government, laying its Foundation on such Principles, and organizing its Powers in such Form, as to them shall seem most likely to effect their Safety and Happiness."

Notwithstanding the impressive theoretical grounding of the Declaration of Independence, however, its author was a profoundly practical man, as indeed were nearly all the leading figures in the American Revolution. This distinguishes the American especially from the French Revolution, which began thirteen years later. Thomas Jefferson, James Madison, George Washington, Alexander Hamilton, John Adams, Benjamin Franklin, and James

Wilson, to name only the most important, had among them long experience in political life and the practice of law, including crafting state constitutions. They were deeply learned in English history, political history generally, and the history of political thought back to Aristotle and Plato. References to Cicero, Tacitus, and Plutarch dot their pages, along with frequent allusions to republics as diverse as Venice, Holland, Geneva, Sparta, and Rome. They were not mere theoreticians, as the fruits of their labors have attested for more than two centuries. Nowhere was their capacity as statesmen so clearly demonstrated as in their greatest achievement, the Constitution of the United States.

This document is significant in a number of respects for anyone interested in the foundations of liberal political orders. The document itself was drafted in Philadelphia in the summer of 1787, by a Constitutional Convention composed of fifty-five delegates sent by the state legislatures. It was submitted to the states for public debate, and was eventually ratified in 1788 when approved by nine of the original thirteen states, and eventually by all. Some of the most interesting political documents ever written are the short essays published in popular newspapers during the debate over ratification. Some approved and others argued against the proposed Constitution, but papers on both sides reveal the degree of reflection and wisdom that animated this experiment in self-government. In fact, in the first of a series of proconstitutional essays called *The Federalist Papers*, Alexander Hamilton called attention to the uniqueness of what was being attempted in the American experiment. "It seems to have been reserved for the people of this country," he wrote, "by their conduct and example, to decide the important question, whether societies of men are really capable or not of establishing good government from reflection and choice, or whether they are forever destined to depend for their political constitutions on accident and force. If there be any truth in the remark, the crisis at which we are arrived may with propriety be regarded as the era in which that decision is to be made; and a wrong election of the part we shall act may, in this view, deserve to be considered as the general misfortune of mankind."[3]

The first important contribution is actually the document itself, because excepting the American state constitutions, it was the first written constitution in the world, the first time an entire nation had laid out its plan of government in written form. And although it took nearly fifteen years after ratification to see the significance of this, its importance is more than symbolic. In 1803, in a great legal case settled by the U. S. Supreme Court, the supremacy of this written constitution over any other kind of law was established for the first time. Chief Justice John Marshall, in

[3] Alexander Hamilton, *The Federalist Papers* (New York: New American Library, 1961), No. 1, p. 33.

that famous case, *Marbury v. Madison*, explained the importance of this idea:

> That the people have an original right to establish, for
> their future government, such principles, as, in their opin-
> ion, shall most conduce to their own happiness is the basis
> of which the whole American fabric has been erected. The
> exercise of this original right is a very great exertion; nor
> can it, nor ought it, to be frequently repeated. The princi-
> ples, therefore, so established, are deemed fundamental.
> And as the authority from which they proceed is supreme,
> and can seldom act, they are designed to be permanent.
>
> This original and supreme will organizes the govern-
> ment, and assigns to different departments their respective
> powers. It may either stop here, or establish certain limits
> not to be transcended by those departments.
>
> The government of the United States is of the latter
> description. The powers of the legislature are defined and
> limited; and that those limits may not be mistaken, or for-
> gotten, the constitution is written. To what purpose are
> powers limited, and to what purpose is that limitation
> committed to writing, if these limits may, at any time, be
> passed by those intended to be restrained? The distinction
> between a government with limited and unlimited
> powers is abolished, if those limits do not confine the per-
> sons on whom they are imposed, and if acts prohibited
> and acts allowed, are of equal obligation. It is a proposi-

tion too plain to be contested, that the constitution controls any legislative act repugnant to it; or, that the legislature may alter the constitution by an ordinary act.

Between these alternatives there is no middle ground. The constitution is either a superior paramount law, unchangeable by ordinary means, or it is on a level with ordinary legislative acts, and like other acts, is alterable when the legislature shall please to alter it.

If the former part of the alternative be true, then a legislative act contrary to the constitution is not law: if the latter part be true, then written constitutions are absurd attempts, on the part of the people, to limit a power in its own nature illimitable.[4]

Marshall's decision established the great principle that the written Constitution is not an absurd attempt, but is instead more fundamental than any governmental decision, even by the legislature. As one commentator has written, "This principle is wholly and exclusively American. It is America's original contribution to the science of Law."[5]

A second innovative feature of the federal Constitution is its use of federalism, in a large commercial republic, to overcome the problem that had always been the bane of

---

[4] *Readings in American Government,* edited by Nichols and Nichols (Dubuque, Iowa: Kendall/Hunt Publishing Co., 1990), p. 295.

[5] Albert J. Beveridge, *The Life of John Marshall* (Boston: Houghton Mifflin Co., 1919), Vol III, p. 142.

democratic republics, namely, factions. The most common factions have always been the rich and the poor, though religious and other kinds of factions are also dangerous. In a famous argument in the tenth *Federalist Paper*, James Madison suggested that there is no way to eliminate factions in a republic, unless you extinguish liberty and force all citizens to think alike. But he suggested that the large American federal republic offered a way to solve the problem of factions anyway. In a large, diverse republic, he said, so many divisions or factions will exist that no faction will be able to gain power and oppress others. Instead of the haves and have-nots likely to be the main factions in a small republic, in a large and diverse republic, the kinds of haves and have-nots will be so numerous that they will be unlikely to feel themselves to be part of a simple faction. Those who are rich farmers will be as likely to join forces with other farmers as with rich merchants, whose interests may be quite different. And thus, Madison said, instead of trying to eliminate factions, a large republic—with many regions and many interests— actually will be saved by the proliferation of factional interests, since none is able to become a majority. It was a brilliant piece of reasoning, and has proven Madison's genius, for American society has not fallen victim to the factional strife that destroyed so many small republics over the centuries.

Many other features of the American Constitution could be mentioned here, but the focus will be on just one: the mechanism designed to address a problem noted before, namely how to limit the power of government in practice. Madison, again, explained the problem. The Constitution makes use of the notion of separation of powers, dividing governmental powers among three branches: legislative, executive, and judicial. Each of the branches was made as independent as possible from control or influence of the other branches, because, as Madison wrote, "The accumulation of all powers, legislative, executive, and judiciary, in the same hands, whether of one, a few, or many, and whether hereditary, self-appointed, or elective, may justly be pronounced the very definition of tyranny."[6] But no government would be workable if the branches were simply separate. The legislature, for example, might pass a law but the executive refuse to enforce it. Madison insists that unless these departments be "so far connected and blended as to give each a constitutional control over the others, the degree of separation which the maxim requires, as essential to a free government, can never in practice be duly maintained."[7] But what will prevent two branches from combining to oppress the third, and the people as well? The framers were practical men,

[6] Madison, *Federalist Papers,* No. 47, p. 301.
[7] *Ibid.,* No. 48, p. 308.

and they knew that "a mere demarcation on parchment of the constitutional limits of the several departments is not a sufficient guard against those encroachments which lead to a tyrannical concentration of all the powers of the government in the same hands."[8]

They considered other precautions—such as periodic constitutional conventions—but decided that for various reasons they would not be effective. "To what expedient, then, shall we finally resort, for maintaining in practice the necessary partition of power among the several departments as laid down in the Constitution? The only answer that can be given is that as all these exterior provisions are found to be inadequate the effect must be supplied, by so contriving the interior structure of the government as that its several constituent parts may, by their mutual relations, be the means of keeping each other in their proper places."[9] And this, Madison claims, the Constitution succeeds in doing: "The great security against a gradual concentration of the several powers in the same department consists in giving to those who administer each department the necessary constitutional means and personal motives to resist encroachments of the others. The provision for defense must in this, as in all other cases, be made commensurate to the danger of attack. Ambition must be

---

[8] *Ibid.,* No. 48, p. 313.

[9] *Ibid.,* No. 51, p. 320.

made to counteract ambition. The interest of the man must be connected with the constitutional rights of the place."[10]

The framers' hopes were grounded on what Madison calls "the policy of supplying, by opposite and rival interests, the defect of better motives."[11] He admits that "it may be a reflection on human nature that such devices should be necessary to control the abuses of government. But what is government itself but the greatest of all reflections on human nature? If men were angels, no government would be necessary. If angels were to govern men, neither external nor internal controls on government would be necessary. In framing a government which is to be administered by men over men, the great difficulty lies in this: you must first enable the government to control the governed; and in the next place oblige it to control itself."[12] Thus, as an extra precaution the Constitution divides the legislature—expected to be the most powerful and dangerous branch—into two different houses, and even more, seeks to "render them, by different modes of election and different principles of action, as little connected with each other as the nature of their common functions and their common dependence on the society will admit."[13] The

[10] *Ibid.,* No. 51, p. 321.

[11] *Ibid.,* p. 322.

[12] *Ibid.*

[13] *Ibid.*

framers anticipated competition among the political leaders, with no branch willing to let itself be dominated by
another. As a result of this complicated balance, it was
hoped, the federal government would be unable to enact
any policies not agreed on by a majority of the various
factions that make up the body of citizens.

One more mechanism for protecting individual rights
should be mentioned, though it was not part of the original Constitution. It is the famous Bill of Rights, added
during the first two years of the republic at the insistence
of some who still feared the power of the federal government. The Bill of Rights explicitly denies to the government the power to interfere with specific individual
freedoms. "Congress shall make no law," the First
Amendment states, "Respecting an establishment of religion, or abridging the freedom of speech, or of the press,
or the right of the people peaceably to assemble, and to
petition the government for a redress of grievances." The
government may not take private property for public use
without just compensation, may not abridge the right of
a citizen to a speedy and public trial, and so on. These
guarantees have protected Americans from government
interference for two hundred years, and are sometimes
regarded as the clearest symbol of the United States's
commitment to individual rights and limited government.
Laws passed by the Congress, or by the states, have been
overturned on review by the courts if they are found to

violate the rights guaranteed in the Constitution. Thus the power of the government to oppress has been limited, in practice, not only by disagreements and competition among the three branches, but by the American understanding that there are rights that the government may not violate even with the best of intentions. This is the core of liberal individualism, and the foundation for both the U. S. Constitution and the system of government that derives from it.

Chapter 13

MAJORITY TYRANNY

We have traced the philosophical roots of liberal commercial society both to the thinkers who contributed to
the liberal understanding of human nature and politics
and to the practices of the past which helped to prepare
the ground for liberal societies. The starting point was a
brief look at the roots of liberalism in ancient Greece and
early Christianity, after which we examined historical
sources in England's emergence from feudalism and in the
Protestant Reformation. We investigated the new views of
man and of nature found in early modern philosophers
such as Machiavelli, Bacon, and Hobbes. In the ideas of
John Locke, Montesquieu, David Hume, and Adam Smith
we have seen the fully developed account of the liberal
understanding of man and society. Finally, in the previous
chapter, which dealt with the American founders and the
U. S. Constitution, we arrived at the dawn of what might

be called the liberal century, the nineteenth century. In the American experience we saw the fullest practical example of a liberal commercial society, complete with a written constitution and the framework of federalism. In such a society we find secure individual rights, limited government powers, and men and women free to seek their fortunes, material or otherwise, as they choose.

As the American experience makes clear, liberal commercial societies have generated prosperity and technological development unimaginable even a century ago. That the material progress of these societies is connected to freedom, not just economic freedom but intellectual and spiritual freedom as well, is manifest in the fact that nations with other political systems—even where science is encouraged and supported—lag far behind the progress generated by free individuals. Free individuals, making their own decisions about how to employ resources and property, are the hallmark of a liberal commercial society. The few nations of Asia that have in the last two decades enjoyed unprecedented economic growth under free enterprise capitalism have clearly shown the connection between individual freedom, the rule of law, and economic progress.

And note that the unheard of prosperity of the United States has also been accompanied—despite what many detractors say—by greater equality than in any other type of society, today or in the past. Any American can shop in any store, work where his abilities permit, work as hard as he wants, save or spend as he chooses. This does not mean everyone is rich, but in the United States no one is protected by privilege of class or party. Not too long ago the richest man in the United States was a man named Sam Walton who developed a chain of discount stores and became a billionaire. He came from humble origins, lived in a small town in Oklahoma, and drove a pickup truck. Thousands of immigrants pour into the United States every month from Asia, Mexico, and Central America. Many speak no English, but somehow they are able to find work, and within a generation their children may be entering medical, engineering, and law schools and living as full members of their adopted society. What brings these people? And why are they outspoken defenders and proponents of American liberties and opportunities? The answer is obvious.

But this favorable picture of liberal commercial societies would be incomplete without mention of the dangers and problems that confront them. Every kind of society confronts dangers to its existence—including other kinds of regimes that deny its legitimacy. But liberal commercial societies almost from their beginnings have had to struggle with what might be called internal dangers. One such internal danger—a new sort of majority tyranny—became a serious concern for political philosophers in the middle of the nineteenth century.

The general problem of majority tyranny is of course

as old as democratic government itself. But large modern democratic republics seemed to make possible a new kind of majority tyranny, a kind never before seen. The reasons for this were most cogently explained in the 1830s by a young Frenchman, Alexis de Tocqueville, who traveled to America to study the political order he believed would sooner or later come to the entire world.

The most striking feature of American society, according to Tocqueville, was something he called "equality of conditions." By this he meant the absence of barriers based on blood or hereditary privilege. In America there was no hereditary aristocracy with distinctive tastes and inclinations. "It is not that in the United States, as everywhere, there are no rich," he said, "indeed I know of no other country where love of money has such a grip on men's hearts or where stronger scorn is expressed for the theory of permanent equality of property."[1] According to Tocqueville this meant, among other things, that all the members of such a society tend toward a middling level in attainments, including education: "I think there is no other country in the world where, proportionately to population, there are so few ignorant and so few learned individuals as in America."[2] In America there is no learned class, with authority in political and moral matters based

[1] Alexis de Tocqueville, *Democracy in America*, edited by J. P. Mayer and translated by George Lawrence (New York: Harper & Row, 1969), p. 54.

[2] *Ibid.,* p. 55.

on a lifetime of study and reflection. Thus Americans consider themselves all more or less equal in their judgment.
But since no human being can discover for himself all the
truths he must make use of in everyday life, men living in
times of equality are forced to rely, for authoritative opinions, on "what most people say." As Tocqueville explained,
"when standards are unequal and men unalike, there are
some very enlightened and learned individuals whose
intelligence gives them great power, while the multitude
is very ignorant and blinkered. As a result men living
under an aristocracy are naturally inclined to be guided in
their views by a more thoughtful man or class, and they
have little inclination to suppose the masses infallible. In
times of equality the opposite happens. The nearer men
are to a common level of uniformity, the less are they
inclined to believe blindly in any man or any class. But
they are readier to trust the mass, and public opinion
becomes more and more mistress of the world."[3] This is
the new kind of majority tyranny, a tyranny of the majority over thought, which Tocqueville foresaw as a special
problem in large democratic republics whose hallmark is
equality of conditions.

The most famous response to the problem of "tyranny
of the majority over thought" was formulated by the
British philosopher John Stuart Mill. Mill was profoundly

[3] *Ibid.,* p. 435.

influenced by Tocqueville—indeed he wrote lengthy introductory essays to each of Tocqueville's volumes when they were first published in English, and he asked Tocqueville to write articles for the journal of opinion he edited. Mill's celebrated suggestion for protecting individuals from the heavy pressure to conform to the majority view was formulated in a work called *On Liberty*, published in 1859. It is a surprising work in some respects because its prescriptions seem so different from recommendations Mill made in some other writings (both earlier and later).

The central argument of *On Liberty* depends on a distinction between the conduct of an individual that affects only himself, which Mill calls self-regarding conduct, and other-regarding conduct, that which affects the interests of others. Mill starts by admitting that "everyone who receives the protection of society owes a return for the benefit, and the fact of living in society renders it indispensable that each should be bound to observe a certain line of conduct towards the rest."[4] Society has the right to prevent anyone from injuring the interests of another—at least certain interests "which, either by express legal provision, or by tacit understanding, ought to be considered as rights."[5] Society also has the right to require each person to bear "his share (to be fixed on some equitable

[4] John Stuart Mill, *On Liberty* (New York: Norton & Co., 1975), p. 70.
[5] *Ibid.*

principle) of the labours and sacrifices incurred for defending the society or its members from injury and molestation. These conditions society is justified in enforcing, at all costs to those who endeavour to withhold fulfillment."[6] Society may regulate individual conduct in these two respects, but strictly speaking society may not—through laws and penalties—do more than this to regulate individual conduct. Purely self-regarding conduct is, or should be, of no concern to society.

What is most clearly outside the bounds of government regulation, according to Mill, is the realm of speech and opinion. The expression of mere opinions, Mill argues, can harm no one. The suppression of any point of view is unjustifiable because to suppress an opinion is to claim a monopoly on truth, which no one possesses. The power to control the expression of opinion, then, is illegitimate. "The best government has no more title to it than the worst," Mill says. "It is as noxious, or more noxious, when exerted in accordance with public opinion, than when in opposition to it. If all mankind minus one were of one opinion, and only one person were of the contrary opinion, mankind would be no more justified in silencing that one person, than he, if he had the power, would be justified in silencing mankind."[7]

It is not merely *unjust* to suppress opinions but also

[6] *Ibid.*

[7] *Ibid.*, p. 18.

unwise or even dangerous, according to Mill. "The pecu-
liar evil of silencing the expression of an opinion is, that it
is robbing the human race; posterity as well as the existing generation; those who dissent from the opinion, still
more than those who hold it. If the opinion is right, they
are deprived of the opportunity of exchanging error for
truth: if wrong, they lose, what is almost as great a benefit, the clearer perception and livelier impression of truth,
produced by its collision with error."[8] Thus there are two
branches to his argument: "We can never be sure that the
opinion we are endeavoring to stifle is a false opinion; and
if we were sure, stifling it would be an evil still."[9]

Mill's arguments for complete freedom of speech are
probably the most famous portion of *On Liberty*, and are
widely accepted in societies such as the United States,
where the legal system in recent decades has refused to
permit even democratically elected legislatures to go very
far in curtailing speech, including speech deemed offensive or obscene by a large majority. Of course, no freedom
is absolutely without some limit, and, as Mill himself
admitted, "even opinions lose their immunity when the
circumstances in which they are expressed are such as to
constitute their expression a positive instigation to some
mischievous act. An opinion that corn-dealers are starvers
of the poor, or that private property is robbery, ought to

[8] *Ibid.*
[9] *Ibid.*

be unmolested when simply circulated through the press, but may justly incur punishment when delivered orally to an excited mob assembled before the house of a corn-dealer, or when handed about among the same mob in the form of a placard."[10] But of course speech in such a circumstance can readily be considered to be something other than mere words, and thus to fall into the category of action or conduct, which Mill concedes may be regulated by society.

Mill's arguments about the regulation of individual *conduct* are, in the end, more problematic than his defense of freedom of expression. What seems at first a clear distinction—between self-regarding and other-regarding conduct—appears to break down as Mill discusses it further. In Mill's attempt to protect "non-conforming" individuality, he at first insists that society should tolerate any sort of behavior, no matter how deviant from the norm, so long as it injures no one but the individual himself. "As soon as any part of a person's conduct affects prejudicially the interests of others, society has jurisdiction over it, and the question whether the general welfare will or will not be promoted by interfering with it, becomes open to discussion. But there is no room for entertaining any such question when a person's conduct affects the interests of no persons besides himself, or need not affect them unless

[10] *Ibid.,* p. 53.

they like (all the persons concerned being of full age, and the ordinary amount of understanding). In all such cases, there should be perfect freedom, legal and social, to do the action and stand the consequences."[11]

But such "perfect freedom," he concedes, may be the object of "moral reprobation" amounting to social ostracism, if the individual's conduct is marked by vice and degeneracy—even though injurious only to himself. "There is a degree of folly, and a degree of what may be called (though the phrase is not unobjectionable) lowness or depravation of taste, which, though it cannot justify doing harm to the person who manifests it renders him necessarily and properly a subject of distaste, or, in extreme cases, even of contempt: a person could not have the opposite qualities in due strength without entertaining these feelings. Though doing no wrong to any one, a person may so act as to compel us to judge him, and feel to him, as a fool, or as a being of an inferior order."[12] But this surely throws us back upon the problem of majority tyranny over thought, at least thought that concerns the questions of morality and the proper way to live. "A person who shows rashness, obstinacy, self-conceit—who cannot live within moderate means—who cannot restrain himself from hurtful indulgences—who pursues animal

[11] *Ibid.*, p. 70.
[12] *Ibid.*, p. 72.

pleasures at the expense of those of feeling and intellect—
must expect to be lowered in the opinion of others, and
to have a less share of their favourable sentiments."[13]
Nonetheless Mill insists that the "distinction between the
loss of consideration which a person may rightly incur by
defect of prudence or of personal dignity, and the reprobation which is due to him for an offence against the
rights of others, is not a merely nominal distinction."[14]

Mill himself anticipates that "many readers will refuse
to admit" his distinction. "How (it may be asked) can any
part of the conduct of a member of society be a matter of
indifference to the other members?"[15] Must we not admit
that society has some duty to educate its members about
how to live properly? Mill does not deny this; indeed he
suggests that precisely because social influence is so powerful during an individual's formative years, society must
not exercise coercion on an individual once he is grown.
"Armed not only with all the powers of education, but
with the ascendancy which the authority of a received
opinion always exercises over the minds who are least
fitted to judge for themselves; and aided by the *natural*
penalties which cannot be prevented from falling on those
who incur the distaste or the contempt of those who
know them; let not society pretend that it needs, besides

[13] *Ibid.,* pp. 72–73.
[14] *Ibid.,* p. 74.
[15] *Ibid.*

all this, the power to issue commands and enforce obedience in the personal concerns of individuals, in which, on
all principles of justice and policy, the decision ought to
rest with those who are to abide the consequences."[16]
Though he was careful not to say it too directly, Mill was
probably most concerned about religious bigotry—
indeed he mentions in this context the "fanatical moral
intolerance of the Puritans" of an earlier century. In Mill's
view, the "strongest of all arguments against the interference of the public with purely personal conduct is that,
when it does interfere, the odds are that it interferes
wrongly, and in the wrong place."[17]

Even though in some areas his distinctions are not
clear, John Stuart Mill's *On Liberty* must be regarded as a
salutary attempt to resist the sort of paternalistic tyranny
that had been feared by Tocqueville.

In the concluding section Mill formulates three objections to government intrusion into affairs beyond its
direct functions of protecting the security and property of
citizens. The first is that some things are simply done
better by individuals than by a government, however well
intentioned. The second is that "in many cases, though
individuals may not do the particular thing so well, on the
average, as the officers of government, it is nevertheless

[16] *Ibid.*, p. 77.
[17] *Ibid.*, p. 78.

desirable that it should be done by them, rather than by the government, as a means to their own mental education—a mode of strengthening their active faculties, exercising their judgment, and giving them a familiar knowledge of the subjects with which they are thus left to deal."[18] He offers as examples the very things Tocqueville had discussed, such as serving on juries or participating in local institutions. But Mill goes even further here, in a passage that is important to the libertarians of later generations: "The third and most cogent reason for restricting the interference of government is the great evil of adding unnecessarily to its power. Every function superadded to those already exercised by the government causes its influence over hopes and fears to be more widely diffused, and converts, more and more, the active and ambitious part of the public into hangers-on of the government, or of some party which aims at becoming the government. If the roads, the railways, the banks, the insurance offices, the great joint-stock companies, the universities, and the public charities, were all of them branches of government; if in addition, the municipal corporations and local boards, with all that now devolves on them, became departments of the central administration; if the employees of all these different enterprises were appointed and paid by the government, and looked to the government

[18] *Ibid.*, p. 101.

for every rise in life; not all the freedom of the press and popular constitution of the legislature would make this or any other country free otherwise than in name."[19] Many people will recognize Mill's depiction as an apt description of most societies—especially socialist ones—in the century just gone by, the century not of freedom but of statism, all across the globe.

[19] *Ibid.*, p. 102.

Chapter 14

FREE SOCIETIES
AND THE FUTURE

The third millennium is upon us, and quite naturally this provokes reflections on the prospects for free societies. Such societies have never been common, and for most of this past century they have been threatened—whether in actual wars or the Cold War—by the totalitarian or state-centered systems of communism and fascism. The crucial event of the final years of the twentieth century was, without doubt, the collapse of communism. The demise of the Soviet Union, and, in communist China, at least some degree of economic liberalization, changed the picture quite radically. The virtual disappearance of the sworn enemies of liberal democracy ("We will bury you!" Nikita Kruschev threatened) should mean, for free societies, the end of the burden and expense of defending themselves against hostile regimes. It is possible to argue that there is today no serious alternative to liberal democracy as the proper form of social organization—and arguments of this kind, though advanced for nearly two centuries, do not seem as implausible as they did a few short years ago.[1] Thus the prospects for free societies ought to be quite good.

In other respects as well the situation of free societies seems favorable. In terms of material prosperity, free societies have continued to make progress in recent decades, and at no time in history have so many people enjoyed security and relative leisure. Medical science has helped to prolong human life and to keep us generally healthier. Technological developments that would have amazed earlier generations now make it possible to enjoy a symphony performance in our home, "talk" electronically to someone half a world away, or call for help in an emergency from a remote mountain or the middle of an ocean. These prodigies of technological advance in communications and computers are commonplace today; who knows what the next decades will bring?

Yet there are plenty of indications that the times are not as good as they ought to be for free societies. Complaints of moral decay and economic stagnation persist, and the complaints are not without merit. The condition of the inner cities in the United States, with their population of what is now called the "underclass," is cause for alarm. The

---

[1] Francis Fukuyama, *The End of History and the Last Man* (New York: The Free Press, 1992).

liberal democracies of Europe are experiencing stagnant economies and declining populations—and the latter is historically, at least, a sure sign of decline. The educational attainments of students in the United States are abysmal, and even repeated lowering of the standards (itself a sign of decline) has failed to persuade parents and other observers that all is well. Signs of decadence in art abound—not just in the fine arts, but in popular entertainment as well, where ever more brutal, violent, and pornographic films (and music) corrode our sensibilities. And on top of everything else a large chunk of the educated elites or intellectuals in Western societies are unhappy or, as it is sometimes put, "alienated" from the beliefs of the majority and the institutions that embody their views, including the churches.

Moreover, even in free societies, there is less freedom than there ought to be, according to many citizens. Among the reasons for the Republican sweep in the 1994 congressional elections was surely the vociferous complaints from all around the country of violations of property rights by government officials, and especially those of the federal government. College campuses have made efforts to restrict speech—offensive speech, as the administrators put it—in order to ensure that no one is made uncomfortable by the views of others. Sensitivity training is prescribed for anyone who offends. And the increasing number of pages in the *Federal Register* is one commonly cited measure of the degree to which we are increasingly regulated and restricted in vast areas of life—transportation, health care, occupational conditions, the renting of apartments, hiring, even expressions of religious faith.

I.

The question of why even free societies seem to be less free than they should be (or than many believe they should be) is worth a little consideration, since it bears on the issue of the future of free society. Recent political events in the United States, going back to at least 1980, suggest that we may be witnessing the turning of a tide that for nearly a century had been running in the direction of ever-larger government. Historian Paul Johnson has argued persuasively that the twentieth century should properly be regarded as the "century of the state." "The state was the great gainer of the twentieth century; and the central failure. Up to 1914, it was rare for the public sector to embrace more than 10 per cent of the economy; by the 1970s, even in liberal countries, the state took up to 45 per cent of the GNP."[2] The political transformation that began (in the United States) in the 1930s in the faith or hope that state action could make human beings better

---

[2] Paul Johnson, *Modern Times: The World from the Twenties to the Eighties* (New York: Harper and Row, 1983), p. 729. Cf. p. 14, and Karl Deutsch, "The Crisis of the State," in *Government and Opposition* (London School of Economics), summer 1981.

off and protect them from the things they fear seems to have run its course: more and More voices decry the size of government, the burden of taxation, and the bureaucratic intrusions of an endless list of agencies of the welfare state, to which our representatives have granted power over our daily lives.

What gave rise to such faith and hope that government could improve our lives in the first place? That is harder to say, but almost certainly it was related to an excessive faith in the power of the social sciences.[3] The clearest case is the science of economics, as presented in the theories of John Maynard Keynes, who persuaded generations of scholars and politicians that wise human beings, with the right information, could "fine-tune" economic arrangements through government policies and central banking decisions, and thus improve the lives of human beings. Sociology, criminology, psychology, and political science developed similar cases of hubris.

The social sciences can be identified as a source of the ills of free societies in another way as well. For there can be little doubt that social science has contributed to the increasingly widespread view that human beings are not fully responsible—perhaps scarcely responsible at all—for their actions. If, as it teaches, each human being is to be understood as a product of his environment and upbringing (and surely it is

---

[3] The suggestion is also made by Johnson, *Modern Times.*

unfair to hold someone responsible for his own upbringing), then we will be more and more inclined to excuse
or ignore behavior once regarded as offensive, reckless, or
even criminal. Far too many people, for example, take it
for granted that crime is the result of poverty. The
Menendez brothers in Los Angeles were acquitted of
killing their parents, even though they admitted shooting
them, on the grounds that their parents had abused them.

The decline in individual responsibility has another
source, namely, the decline in religious belief (or, in many
cases, the transformation of religious faith into a kind of
"secular faith" in social relief projects). If people either
don't go to church or understand the church mainly as a
relief agency devoted to helping the poor, the hungry, the
oppressed, and the less fortunate, they will probably begin
to lose sight of the spiritual teachings of the church. Thus
they cease to some degree to see themselves as free beings
created in God's image and responsible for the choice of
good or evil. They may also begin to lose sight of the traditional Judeo-Christian teaching of the sanctity of the
individual human life in the eyes of God, and thus be
open to suggestions about suicide, euthanasia, or abortion,
where the value of life is measured in a calculus involving
suffering, benefit, even convenience, or what is sometimes
called the quality of life. The result is the cheapening of
life itself, a cheapening that we see reflected in entertainment and in the lyrics of popular music. All seem to be

symptoms of moral decay, and as such cause for concern about free societies.

Alongside statism, the decline of responsibility, and other symptoms of moral decay is another and more subtle, even paradoxical, ill that besets free societies. It is paradoxical because free societies are in general liberal democratic societies, and the ill is (or stems from) democracy itself—perhaps we can call it a democratic excess. In any case, it is an ill to which democracies have a natural tendency. The ill is egalitarianism.

As Tocqueville pointed out in his masterful analysis in *Democracy in America*, there is inevitable tension between liberty and equality in democratic societies. The two can coexist, of course, but sometimes the desire for equality becomes so powerful that in order to foster it, liberties are curtailed. Equality of opportunity, in these circumstances, begins to be the object of complaints, and gives way to equality of results. This can be seen in small ways all around us. Those who succeed most in the production of wealth, for example, are taxed punitively, as a form of redistribution to help those who are less successful. Something of this sort has been a problem in democracies since ancient times. Commentators beginning with Aristotle have observed that democracies are prone to the vice of envy and therefore susceptible to class-based politics, in which the poor are pitted against the rich. Concerning fiscal or tax policy, this problem of envy may be a relatively minor issue. But in a deeper way, the impulses of egalitarianism can undermine the attitudes on which liberty itself depends. The striving for excellence, which can always be seen where individuals have real freedom, will be curtailed, by government authority if necessary, when demands for equality become too shrill.

In college and university admissions, we hear today about practices such as "race-norming," which means applying different standards to members of different racial groups (often in the name of diversity), but which invariably results in the lowering of standards of excellence. If Harvard admits students whose scores are lower than those usually accepted, either some proportion of the students thus admitted will fail, or the general standards must be lowered to ensure that this does not happen. The effects are clear, if we think of the example of athletics, one of the few realms of achievement where sheer talent and ability still seem to be the only criteria for success. We do not hear arguments that teams should reflect the racial mix of society at large, or that racial "diversity" should be taken into account when team members are chosen. Do we care about excellence in athletics more than in academic achievement? Or are different standards acceptable in academic life because of an unspoken assumption that there are no objective criteria (criteria on which we can agree) for excellence in academic achievement?

In secondary education today there is a movement away

from programs for the gifted and talented, and the reason often given is that resources should be devoted to the slower students who need more help. Egalitarianism has even crept into the language: in the name of sensitivity, we are no longer supposed to describe someone—for example someone who is blind, or quadriplegic—as "handicapped" (much less as "crippled"), but as "differently abled." The old-fashioned view that it is desirable in human life to be able to exercise the highest capacities to the fullest extent (with the implication that some inequalities are irremediable) is thus replaced by the view that there is no "highest" or "fullest," only capacities or abilities that are "different." Egalitarianism is here carried to its logical conclusion (some would see this as a *reductio ad absurdum*).

The ills of equality or egalitarianism are probably inevitable in free societies. But it is important to distinguish this problem from the problems of moral decay and statism discussed above, because the remedy, if there is one, must be sought in a different place. Let us turn to the question of remedies for our ills, and in the process put together a summary of the fundamental principles of free societies, based on the discussion in the preceding chapters.

II.

The principles that underlie free societies—the roots of freedom, properly speaking—are modern, as we have repeatedly seen, even though anticipated in ideas from

Greek antiquity and in some of the doctrines of the ancient Christians. As Pericles's Funeral Oration suggests, the Athenians, at least, flirted with the notion of individualism. And the Christian teaching about the sanctity of each individual human life, or the idea that Caesar's realm is to be distinguished from God's realm, could be described as early glimpses of principles important to liberty. However, these ideas begin to play an important role only beginning about the seventeenth century, because such anticipations were easily overshadowed by the core of the classical understanding of the human situation: that man is political by nature, and therefore that his primary duty is to the political community to which he owes his very humanity, and that the aim of political life is excellence or virtue. History at least suggests that where these ideas are paramount, free societies cannot develop and individual freedom cannot flourish.

The first real steps toward a free society were located in the process by which northwest European peoples began to escape the bondage of the feudal system (chapter 4). These steps can be summed up as the development of the rule of law, an independent judiciary, and individual (private or family) ownership of property. These three are found in every society that can properly be described as a free society, and together they form the basic foundation of liberty. The idea of limiting the power of one individual over another—much less of government over individuals—is impossible without law, judges separate from executives or military leaders, and property (without which any individual can be tyrannized because his livelihood is subject to decisions by whoever holds power).

Genuine liberty also requires that spiritual authority be separated from authority over worldly or secular matters, an idea traced here (in imperfect form) to the Protestant Reformation, along with the suggestion that in regard to what matters most, all individuals stand equal to one another, and are not subordinated in a hierarchy to natural superiors. At the time of the Reformation, and even during the settling of Puritan communities in the New World, these principles remained ideals—seeds that would take time and would need new soil in which to grow. That soil, to continue the metaphor, was the product of the "modern project" launched by Machiavelli, who introduced a new view of man and nature, the effect of which was to transform our very understanding of politics.

Liberty, at least individual liberty, cannot develop so long as the political community is regarded as higher in rank than the individual. The modern project challenged this ancient principle by suggesting that human beings are first and foremost individuals, and that political communities are not natural but artificial: they are made by human beings as a means of solving the problems of scarcity and insecurity, which are man's lot as far as mere nature is concerned. This modern view of the purpose of politics meant a serious demotion of politics. Political activity was viewed by the ancient Greeks as one of the highest and most human activities, but in the new view politics is only an instrument, a means of supplying security and making space for individuals to get on with their private business.

The most urgent task for politics, in the modern view as expressed by Machiavelli's follower Thomas Hobbes, is to enable human beings to live in peace. This will be possible, Hobbes suggested, if we view man scientifically. Hobbes suggested ignoring what divides mankind—for example, different conceptions of virtue or of the way to salvation—and focusing instead on what all men have in common, namely, the need to survive. If this is understood to be the goal of politics, then men and women will at least be able to live in peace. Each individual has a right to preserve his life, and once the logic of Hobbes's political science is understood, each will see why he should relinquish some rights (for example, the right to punish someone who threatens him) as long as everyone else does so too, in favor of a sovereign government that will undertake the burden of preserving the peace, promulgating laws, and enforcing them. Thus the new political science introduced the concept of natural rights, which are understood to belong to every individual human being by nature. Some of these rights—such as the right to preserve one's life—are understood to be so fundamental that no government may interfere with them. Governments can be called legitimate only if they rest on the consent (the yielding of natural rights) of the governed. These principles are the basis of all modern liberal constitutionalism.

One other feature of liberal constitutionalism, which has surfaced in the preceding pages at several points, is the separation of powers. This is partly implied in the notion of an independent judiciary, of course, but both Locke and Montesquieu call attention to the advantages of separating legislative from executive power, as a means of limiting government power and protecting individuals against tyranny. When law is made by the same authority responsible for executing or enforcing it, the danger of abuse of power is obviously much greater and, in fact, the rule of law itself is threatened, because the law can be changed at any time to accommodate the wishes of a tyrannical executive. Like the notion of the right of rebellion, which Locke suggested is a protection against the abuse of power, separation of powers does not guarantee liberty, but it goes a long way toward ensuring that governments will respect, in practice, the liberties of individuals.

At the level of foundations, one more set of principles is of the greatest significance. The key is the notion of private property, already mentioned. Once the idea of individualism is accepted, and political communities are understood as means to individual security and happiness, we must consider what happiness means, for most indi-

viduals. What it means, in fact, is prosperity: genuine freedom for most people means not only security but the
chance to live where they want, to marry, raise and support children, provide for their education and a start in
life, and to enjoy the "good things in life"—good food,
music, books, theater and the arts, perhaps the chance to
travel. The enjoyment of such things requires some degree
of wealth or prosperity, and it is no accident that people
flock to places, or countries, where the opportunities are
greatest for the acquisition of wealth. They go not out of
greed but simply out of desire for the good life. Thus we
find that individual freedom is connected to free market
economies, where resources are allocated by market forces
and where individuals cooperate with each other freely
and spontaneously in the production of goods that satisfy
the needs and desires of others (who are therefore willing
to pay for them). This requires free market prices—prices
for labor and goods that are set not by governments or
bureaucrats but by the forces of supply and demand.

What does all this add up to? These principles can be
grouped under three very general headings, although only
for the purpose of a summary:

(1) *Individualism*. This includes the notion that individuals are prior to political communities, or that they have
natural rights—rights independent of belonging to a
community—and that individuals are free and equal in

principle (no one is born with status that gives him authority to rule another).

(2) *Rule of law.* Included here is the notion that political authority is exercised by means of "known and settled laws," to use Locke's phrase, not arbitrary decrees or the whims of a tyrant, and that individuals are judged by judges independent of the military or executive power. Thus, under this heading we include separation of powers.

(3) *Property and commerce.* The right to own property is one of the natural rights governments are instituted to protect. Under this head come all the principles and institutions connected with the generation of wealth: division of labor, free markets or spontaneous cooperation, prices responsive to supply and demand, and free exchange. These in turn require limited government.

III.

Let us consider these principles in the light of our earlier discussion of the ills of free societies. Perhaps a careful consideration of these principles, which are the foundations of a free society, will help remedy the ills. The first of the ills was statism, or the enormous growth during the twentieth century in both the power of the state and in the share of resources, or wealth, consumed or dispensed by state action. This has typically been linked to a hankering for social engineering, or the attempt to change, by government policies, the way people live or the things they believe. Enthusiasm for government seems to have been the product of faith in the social sciences, or the ability of human analysts and planners to identify problems and fix them. But the principles of free market economics suggest that this faith is misplaced: no human wisdom—even if it were always well-intentioned—could be great enough to direct the millions of decision-making human individuals, even in one society, to do what is best for them. Individuals must be allowed to judge for themselves what they wish to do with their talents and resources.

The second of the ills of free societies discussed was moral decay and the decline in individual responsibility. This is a complicated issue, involving among other things a decline in religious belief, which may have no remedy. But a good case can be made that one of the sources of the decline in religious belief—if there is one—is precisely the taking over, by government, of some of the traditional functions of church communities. In the nineteenth century the first source of help for those who fell on hard times was likely to be a church or some other community group—the sort of associations called "intermediate institutions" because they occupy the space between the individual and government. One effect of nearly a century of state growth has been the decline in intermediate institutions. But there is some hope that the discovery of the ineffectiveness of government social engineering will permit us to prune the canopy of state programs and allow some light to reach the lower levels, where churches and community groups grow.

In this study we have traced the outlines of three sets of ideas that are indispensable for free societies. Individualism, or the principle that the individual is prior to the community or state, is one of the core principles of modern thought, but it has been known, and its effects appreciated, for hundreds of years. The principles we grouped under the heading of rule of law (independent judiciary, separation of powers, etc.) are even older, of course, although their greatest development is also the achievement of modern thought. Private property and commerce have always been part of human life, but until the development of political economy in the eighteenth century, commerce was regarded as low, if necessary, and disdained as unworthy of free human beings. Thus the appreciation of these principles is a matter of recovery— of reminding ourselves of their importance.

Yet there is something more. Our times have taught us about a fourth requirement for free society, a requirement that was perhaps not so clear in earlier times because it was taken for granted. This requirement, about which we have learned most in the last one hundred years, is the need for individual moral restraint. What the twentieth century demonstrated was that without this, no legal arrangements, no amount of wealth and prosperity, can protect the freedom of free societies. Some observers regard the problem of declining moral restraint as the direct outgrowth of individualism itself, but a case can be made that it has other roots.

If there really are principles of free society, there must also be something we call human nature: permanent and universal features of human life that enable us to say even so simple a thing as that freedom is desirable for human beings. The intellectual climate of what is called postmodernism has as one of its features the denial that there is anything like the old notion of human nature. But if this tenet is correct, human beings are infinitely malleable, and can't be said to have any permanent needs. One benefit of recalling the principles we have enumerated in this primer is to remind us of the claims of earlier—and perhaps wiser—thinkers about human nature and the good society.

There is one more contribution those older thinkers can make, one not mentioned previously. It is related to the third of the ills of free society, the ill that comes from democracy itself, egalitarianism. One of the great misunderstandings to which we are prone today is the misunderstanding of democracy itself, a regime that we tend to appreciate too much. It is natural for people to think their own ways are best. But democracy means rule by the many or by the people, and as Aristotle for one knew, rule by the many is not inherently more wise or just than rule by other groups: indeed the power of the many often blinds them to their own selfishness. Aristotle classified democracy as one of the bad or selfish regimes, in which rulers (the many) seek their own good at the expense of the good of others. When students discover this teaching in Aristotle's *Politics* they are at first surprised and offended, but for some, at least, the logic of his position is persuasive, and results in a salutary objectivity about democracy that is otherwise too rare. Thus the study of the writings of this ancient political thinker can be valuable to those fortunate enough to live in a free society.

The study of another ancient political philosopher, Plato, can help in a slightly different way. Plato was also concerned about egalitarianism, because equality and liberty can in some circumstances become antagonists. Is there a remedy for this ill? Perhaps. The danger, as Plato presents it in book 8 of *The Republic*, is the tendency toward what we call relativism, the refusal to recognize that some things are higher or better than others, that some ways of life are better or more choiceworthy. A democracy, to use Socrates' words, is "full of freedom and free speech...and where there's license, it's plain that each man would organize his life in it privately just as it pleases him" (557b4-9). This might not be objectionable except for what sometimes follows, namely, the tendency to deny that some things are more noble, or higher, than others. "If someone says that there are some pleasures belonging to fine and good desires and some belonging to bad desires, and that the ones must be practiced and honored and the others checked and enslaved," Socrates suggests, the democratic citizen may not admit it. This Plato identifies as the "life of a man attached to the law of equality," and the danger it poses is that young people come to believe that nothing is high or noble, nothing is worth sacrifice or struggle. And if such views become too widespread, the democratic society can even lose the ability to defend itself—complete relativism is not much of a doctrine to fight for.

The remedy is suggested in the writings of Alexis de Tocqueville. In his examination of the theme of equality in *Democracy in America*, Tocqueville pointed out that in democratic ages, when men and women see themselves as equal, they also tend to feel they are powerless. This affects even the way they study history: democratic historians write as if individuals have no power to shape events or make a difference, and they attribute historical developments to general causes, such as economic trends. In an aristocracy the opposite happens: historians overemphasize the importance of individual actions and decisions. What is most needed in each case, according to Tocqueville, is the truth contained in the kind of history that is not likely to be written: individuals in a democracy need to read aristocratic history in order to feel that individuals can make a difference. They need to read about great men and women, about heroic deeds and great sacrifices, about people who live for what is noble and grand. Such study can act as a remedy for the ill of egalitarianism, the effects of which Plato saw so clearly. Thus, we come to the surprising conclusion that what citizens in a liberal democracy need most is to read the works of the greatest authors and thinkers from undemocratic ages. Perhaps, after all, the ancients can be said to have something to contribute to the principles of free societies. If there are to be free societies, there is no substitute for liberal education.

INDEX